Advance Praise for *Me, Finally*

"From the very first line of *Me, Finally* you'll find yourself beginning to consider a new way of embracing life – a way to be more content in your work, your relationships, and especially with how you feel about yourself."

~ Steve Farrell, Worldwide Coordinating Director, Humanity's Team

"Dr. Mitch Tishler's heart and messages are pure. I encourage everyone to embrace *Me, Finally* and discover his profound offering."

~ Shajen Joy Aziz, best-selling author and creator of *Discover the Gift*

"In his book *Me, Finally: Navigating Life with an Open Heart*, Dr. Mitch Tishler reveals the power of the healing love that flows through his be-ing to all that he encounters. He invites us on a journey to explore 'the medicine in the excruciating'; to view the true stories of our lives; to discover the wholeness and unconditional love that we have always been. The words of the book form a safe container for the journey – a container that is infinitely vast, yet simply present at all times. Reading this book is an experience of healing, of awakening, of discovering, finally, who we are."

~ Karen Wyatt, MD, author of *What Really Matters*

"*Me, Finally* draws you in like a warm blanket wrapping you in its poetry, wisdom, and inspiration. If you are wondering how love works and whether it is worth getting to know, look no further – this book shows you how."

~ Sherianna Boyle, M.Ed., C.A.G.S., author of *Choosing Love*

"*Me, Finally* is a gentle invitation to live as pure, loving awareness and presence in the world. Dr. Mitch Tishler creates a beautiful activation of the homing instinct that leads us deeper into the authentic essence of who we really are. This is a powerful and moving guidebook for anyone open to being, relating, and living in resonance with their heart."

~ Dr. Julie Krull, psychotherapist, host of *The Dr. Julie Show*, and founder of GoodoftheWhole.com

"In his book *Me, Finally* Dr. Mitch Tishler breaks new ground in self-awareness by revealing the true meaning of 'Seeing With Heart' and charting a simple course for each of us to be – Me, Finally. This book will take you on a journey of discovery filled with recurring 'wows' and 'ahas!' Uncovering the true intent will be like turning on a light switch. *Me, Finally* should be openly read and generously shared."

~ Deborah L. Hall, author and speaker of *Million Dollar Moments*

"Reading *Me, Finally*, I instantly started to feel calm in a way that I didn't expect – as though I was actually sitting in a room listening to the wise words of a special soul who was taking me on a magical healing journey inside myself - to a place I didn't want to leave; to a place I instead choose to revisit whenever I'd like to feel more calm or peace in my heart. Mitch has a unique style of writing I've not experienced before – soothing, stimulating, and inviting you to consider different possibilities for reconnecting to the pure essence of who you were born to be. I thoroughly recommend this book, even if you think you've already done your inner work. You will be inspired by what it reveals about yourself and the possibilities ahead. Thanks for writing such a transformational book, Mitch!"

~ Alisoun Mackenzie, author of *Heartatude:*
The 9 Principles of Heart-Centered Success

"*Me, Finally* takes us on a paradigm-shifting journey of healing, calling for each of us to open our hearts to the wisdom of our authentic selves. With gentle skill, Mitch shows us a profound but simple path to cultivating more love, peace, and joy in our lives. I highly recommend reading and sharing this book."

~ Katherine Parker, author of *Resonance Alchemy: Awakening the Tree of Life*

ME, FINALLY

ME, FINALLY

Navigating Life
with an Open Heart

DR. MITCH TISHLER

Love Your Life

Love Your Life

Love Your Life Publishing
Wilmington, DE
www.loveyourlifepublishing.com

ISBN: 978-1-934509-80-7
Library of Congress Control Number: 2015931350

Printed in the United States of America
First Printing

Front cover design by Dr. Mitch Tishler
Front cover art: The Way of Prayer by Carmelo Blandino, www.blandino.ca
Back cover design by www.2FacedDesign.com
Back cover photo by Brielle Tishler, www.brielletishlerphotography.com
Seeing With Heart logo by Ray Kingston, www.microspective.net
Harmonium video by Chris Blood, www.chrisblood.com
Editing by Gwen Hoffnagle, www.gwenhoffnagle.com

For my dear brother Eric

It is only with the heart that one can see rightly;
what is essential is invisible to the eye.

—Antoine de Saint-Exupery

Contents

Introduction

There are no accidents.

That's what I hear as I listen closely; as I listen to my authentic voice. Like a beacon in the fog, it illuminates the way.

December 28, 1998. It was nighttime. I was driving home. Crossing an intersection, as we often do in our lives, both literally and metaphorically, my car was struck by another traveling at more than fifty miles per hour.

By the time my car came to a stop, I knew that this "accident" wasn't an accident. In fact, as odd as it may seem, I remember having the feeling that something remarkable would come from this "awful" experience.

There were injuries. The most significant was to my right knee, which ultimately required two surgeries. The first was a two-hour procedure and the second took four hours. My intention was to be fully present with my life so I requested to attend both surgeries awake without sedation. The surgeon agreed and regional anesthesia was used. And to further embrace being present, after each procedure I chose not to medicate.

February 27, 2000. The second surgery was far more complex. It required that my leg be in a continuous passive motion (CPM) device beginning immediately the next morning and for six continuous hours per day for the following two months. I really didn't know that my body could experience that extent of "noise." (I consciously choose to use the word *noise* rather than *pain* because we usually associate pain with something bad; there is often judgment around that word.) This noise emanated from my knee and poured out through the rest of my body. It was deafening.

March 4, 2000. Five days after surgery, as I lay on the couch with my leg being moved by the CPM device, something intriguing occurred. I experienced a compelling "feeling" to get a blank piece of paper and take a pen in my left hand – my non-dominant hand. It is interesting to note that my dominant handwriting is essentially illegible, whereas this writing was remarkably legible. Words flowed and poetic writings revealed themselves.

There was no intent to write a book. No conscious awareness of a message. There was simply the compelling feeling to write with my non-dominant hand. A few days into this experience, I heard the name of the collection of writings – Seeing With Heart. I laughed because there was no collection; there were only a few writings. Twelve months later, more than eighty complete handwritten poems had revealed themselves and were sitting in a pile on my closet floor. The majority were written in vertical columns. One was a spiral. And one was even a three-dimensional spherical shape.

At the time I wasn't clear about what was occurring; I just continued to lie on the couch and write. It wasn't until I returned to seeing patients, eighteen months after surgery, that I realized how these writings would support transformational shift. What began to happen was fascinating. A patient would share something troubling and I would realize there was a writing in the collection that directly supported their concern. Later that evening I would shuffle through the pile of writings and find it, photocopy it, and give it to the patient at their next appointment.

Regardless of the patient's issue, there was always a specific writing that was directly helpful. Over time patients began reporting positive shifts in their daily lives, and that they felt the potent medicine contained in these writings. Some were so profoundly moved by this material that they requested to sit down and talk about it more fully. This is how the Seeing With Heart program began.

March 4, 2013. It is now precisely thirteen years later, and I am once again experiencing a compelling feeling to get a blank piece of paper. This time what I "hear" is to share what have become the interpretations of the original writings; to create a book that functions as a self-guided journey for navigating life with an open heart.

Me, Finally is a compilation of actual conversations that emerged as I travelled the Seeing With Heart journey with individuals and groups. The conversations are often verbatim. Others are combinations of several dialogues that speak to a common theme. I am deeply grateful to those who were drawn to listen closely to their authentic voice and embrace Seeing With Heart. It is from their courage to listen to that voice that this body of work has continuously matured.

Their voices appear in italics in the conversations throughout the journey. As you read their responses, you will invariably find yourself reading passages that are very similar to your own personal experiences. In this way, as you read *Me, Finally*, you will directly experience the potent medicine of Seeing With Heart and apply it in your own life. As in the opening line of this book, Seeing With Heart invites us to embrace the possibility that "there are no accidents." Is it an accident that you picked up this book? No. As you read these words, there is an inner feeling of already knowing. You know it is time to listen closely and follow your heart.

Author's Note

To provide you with an experience that most closely resembles the beginning of an authentic Seeing With Heart journey, I prepared a video of myself playing the harmonium – a hand-pumped organ commonly used in traditional Indian music – and chanting *Om namah shivaya (oh-m nah-mah she-vie-ah)* – an ancient Sanskrit phrase that speaks to letting go of those aspects in our lives that are not serving us. Over the years of presenting Seeing With Heart, I've found that incorporating this ancient Sanskrit music into the journey has a deeply calming, potent, heart-opening effect.

The point in the journey at which I pause to play this exquisite music is after paragraph two of Session One. Please don't be concerned if you are unable to view this video, as the journey you are about to embark upon is not dependent on the music. To view the video visit www.mefinally.com/video.

There are also journaling and discussion questions in the Points to Ponder section that you may feel to have alongside while reading. To receive a printable copy of the Points to Ponder and the Seeing With Heart eBook – the complete collection of the original channeled writings – please visit www.mefinally.com/readergift.

Blessings,
Mitch

simply be present

Simply be present
in the infinite moment,
seeing with heart
not listening with head.

The illusion of faces
the texture of many,
lie not from within
but out at the edge.

Listening with head
will herald the fear,
while seeing with heart
embraces the truth.

There are no many,
there is no separation,
there is only the face of the one.

The face of the present
in the infinite moment,
the face of the truth
in the infinite love.

This writing, from March 4th, 2000, was the first from
Seeing With Heart.

Embrace the Possibility

As we begin our journey, Seeing With Heart reminds us that, as on any journey, we may not always know precisely where we are going or where the path is leading. We do not know everything that we will experience, encounter, and see along the way. Seeing With Heart invites us to feel comfortable in that not knowing, recognizing that we make this journey as a compassionate commitment to self – an expression of self-care, of self-love.

To honor that intention, let us gently bring our awareness to our breath and give ourselves permission to stop worrying about all the "stuff" that we "should" be doing, and for the next few moments focus on nothing other than our breath. And as we embrace this meditation, let us open our hearts to the possibility of seeing with other than our ordinary eyes – the possibility of Seeing With Heart.

(At this point in the journey, I pause to play the harmonium. To further enhance your experience, view the video at www.mefinally.com/video.)

How are you feeling?

Peaceful.

Where do you feel that?

In my heart.

So what about the possibility of Seeing With Heart – the possibility of seeing with other than our ordinary eyes? What emotions, sensations, experiences does that evoke?

As I gave myself permission to pause and simply focus on my breath, I felt my whole being welling up and tears came to my eyes. It was very emotional. I'm sensing that there's actually another way to live. There's another way that's even more real; that makes more sense.

Might we invite ourselves to consider that the "welling up and tears" are actually expressions of our natural ways of "be-ing"?

I'm not clear about that and I feel that it will become clear as we go along on our journey.

Yes, it will. Notice that Seeing With Heart asks a lot of questions; that Seeing With Heart is not insistent. It doesn't have the answers. It simply asks questions as a reminder of that which we already know.

That feels really comfortable. I like that Seeing With Heart will be asking questions to help me become clear rather than telling me what to do.

Why is it that when the moon is full the high-water mark moves farther up the beach? Why is it that we don't hear anything when we blow a dog whistle, yet the dog startles? Let these questions be a call to expand our perceptions by closing our eyes and opening our hearts. When we do, we begin to see that there are more connections between us than meet the ordinary eye. We begin to see the invisible threads connecting us all as one. When the moon is full, the invisible thread is reflected in water moving farther up the shoreline. When the dog whistle is blown, the invisible thread is heard by the dog even though we would say that nothing occurred.

What happens when we invite ourselves to consider that there are actually patterns in what appears to be "patternless"? What are these patterns and what are they about? What about the possibility that the occurrences of our lives are never about what they're about? Is there something common to these questions that is at the core of why we often find ourselves feeling unsettled and at times struggle with the myriad of bits and pieces that occur as we move about our lives? Maybe that something has to do with our tendency to interpret our experiences as black or white, bad or good.

Our journey is to explore these questions, and in so doing assemble a framework that provides effective and accessible skills for embracing change, seeing problems as opportunities, gracefully responding rather than overreacting, and letting go. And as we move deeper and deeper from within these possibilities, so we cultivate an expanding experience of inner peace.

Let's consider the invisible threads connecting us all as one, and why we don't see them. Science has established that 80 percent of the information we receive comes in through our eyes. When we compare what the naked eye sees to the notes on a piano, it's as if the eye sees only the eight notes right in the middle of all the notes on a piano. And since 80 percent of our information is received through that lens – the eight notes, Seeing With Heart invites us to consider that our perception of that which we call reality is only based on eight notes when in fact there's a lot more music. The invitation is to expand our spectrums and see and hear and taste and smell and touch the full symphony.

Wow. I never thought of music in that way. This is a very powerful example of how I have limited my life by "playing" with only eight notes.

What might occur when we open up to the fuller symphony?

I have no idea and yet I'm getting a sense that there is so much more.

What drew you to Seeing With Heart?

I thought the phrase "Seeing With Heart" was beautiful and I wanted to learn more.

What is beautiful about the phrase Seeing With Heart?

I feel like that is where I'm going. For example, as a yoga instructor I often prepare and take materials to read to my students during class. The last class I didn't even use the prepared materials. I closed my eyes and went with my heart. It was the most beautiful experience. What flowed out of me was what I really heard; it felt natural, and I felt it couldn't have been more perfect. As I'm talking, I'm learning that that is Seeing With Heart.

And Seeing With Heart is our natural way of be-ing. Let's pause and reflect on what happened when you closed your eyes and opened your heart in a way that to this point you might not have even considered possible.

I listened to my heart and it's amazing what occurred when I did.

As we move along on this journey we will construct a light framework that supports us from falling back into our old repetitive patterns. This framework is comprised of simple building blocks based on easily integrated visual images and metaphors.

To illustrate this point, let's visualize two buildings. Building number one is constructed of stone. Building number two uses post-and-beam construction. The first building requires a significant number of pieces to construct walls, whereas to span a space in the second building requires only three pieces – two posts and one beam. In the second building we can use a curtain to separate the space into two rooms. What's required to get from one room to the other is only a gentle push – a gentle shift in awareness to get through the "fog," whereas in the stone construction we need to remove many stones to create an opening to get through the fog. This example illustrates how the light framework of Seeing With Heart offers a way to easily navigate through the fogs in our lives.

On the Seeing With Heart journey, not only are there specific building blocks to the framework, but these building blocks need to be assembled in a precise sequence. It's like baking a cake; we know that something as simple as not greasing the pan before adding the batter results in a crumbled mess, as I am sure we have all experienced when we skipped a step in our personal lives as well.

And I won't be out in front pulling you along on this journey and saying, "This is the way. When you see it my way, everything is going to be great in your life." Likewise, I won't be behind, pushing you sternly, saying, "Let's go." No – I'm walking along with you.

This journey is about celebrating our humanity and honoring that we all stutter-step and feel wobbly at times. We all do. To stabilize that wobbly experience, Seeing With Heart invites us to have the courage to set off on the path without expectation, even when we don't know where we are going.

At this point in our journey, Seeing With Heart invites us to consider three words: *from within without*. It's really light. It's something easy to carry around in your heart pocket.

from within

From within
the place of
without expectation,
the universe manifests
expanding peace and harmony,
always and in all ways.

When life comes at you, as it has a knack of doing at more than three miles an hour, sometimes more than thirty-three mph, and even at times what feels like more than 3,333 mph – reach into your heart pocket, pull out "from within without," and gently whisper it. These three words remind us about the potent medicine of "being with" what is occurring.

Rather than "Oh, *@!*, I have a flat tire," what about, "I have a flat tire. It's not a preference. I'm not in denial. And there must be something relevant about this, because it happened." We can embrace the possibility of being with the occurrence, accepting it, and not over-reacting by kicking and screaming.

Reflect on recent situations in which either you or someone else unnecessarily overreacted, or when you rationalized, "I could have done this better" or "That didn't go the way it should have," only to feel regretful shortly after.

As basic as "from within without" seems, Seeing With Heart invites us to consider the potent medicine it offers. Using this simple phrase is as basic yet critical as the first step of greasing the pan when baking a cake. However, we can initially feel it's so simple that we find ourselves saying, "Oh, I already know this." What Seeing With Heart suggests is that quite often we don't.

As we move deeper along on our journey, we will find ourselves circling back and revisiting "from within without" as well as other writings to be certain that we are fully embodying the entire Seeing With Heart framework.

the following words

The following words flow as feelings, not thoughts, from the quiet place – the place where all is one. These words are not "mine," yet they have the illusion of flowing through me. Instead, they are core truths that resonate from within each of us. If I felt they were mine, the possibility for receiving them would be not.

To fully know these truths, we must step aside and authentically embrace the possibility of non-ownership. Only in this way are we open to all there is, which is only love, and only then will love flow over all in a way that one only dreams possible.

Now is the time to embrace the possibility – the possibility of Seeing With Heart.

These words revealed themselves six months into the experience of channeling the Seeing With Heart writings. When they showed up it was clear that they were to be page one of the original writings, the opening statement from Seeing With Heart. What they speak to is that the only guru is the guru from within. Seeing With Heart is effective because it's not about me teaching you my way; it's about you making your way.

I'm having an unsettling thought. My mind doesn't want to trust this experience. Initially I was feeling that this was the best program. Now my mind is saying, "This is not true. Mitch is a poet. He wrote these beautiful words and created this program." That's what my mind is saying because that's how I do it. That's all I have known. That's all I have been taught.

It's because we're wired to play on eight notes instead of the entire eighty-eight notes on the piano that we don't readily "see" the full symphony. As we go along on our journey, Seeing With Heart will invite us to consider why we are wired this way, why this is a common pattern, and how to effectively shift.

Okay, as it happens to me often. It's like I am conspiring against myself. I was already beginning to shift and then my mind got in the way.

What about breaking free of that way of being that sees black and white, bad and good?

Yes. It is so limiting.

Seeing With Heart invites us to consider the phrase *"black, white, grey, and blink."*

Let's look at this image. What do you see at the top?

Birds flying.

At the bottom?

Fish swimming.

What are the fish swimming in?

The ocean.

And the birds?

The sky.

So for this example, let's say the fish represent something bad in our lives because in this image they are down in the darkness. And the birds represent something good in our lives because they are above in the light area. As we go about our lives we all know about the black and the white. We often put situations into categories. This is bad and this is good. For example, we're walking down the street and somebody comes at us with a knife. That's black. Likewise, when sharing a compassionate moment with someone we care for, that's white. What do you see in the middle of this image?

I see fish swimming. Oh, but now I see birds flying.

Exactly. The middle of this image represents the gray areas of our lives. It's clear that in the upper portion we are looking at birds flying and in the lower portion we see fish swimming. What we see in the center depends on our perception – how we are gazing at this particular piece of artwork. The center of this image represents the gray areas of our lives – those occurrences that are not quite as clear. "Should I do this or should I do that?"

Isn't it possible that as we are gazing at the "artwork" of our lives, the gray areas – the way we squint and tip our heads to one side or the other – determine our perception? The possibility exists to blink; to actually blink. At times we see fish swimming, and when we blink, without going anywhere, we see birds flying. All it takes is a little blink – a gentle shift. Seeing With Heart is not asking us to move up or down in our lives; it simply invites us to blink and see that there is another option. We don't have to make it better. We don't have to leave our cultural, political, or religious preferences. We don't have to change a situation. The possibility exists to blink and be with that situation, be with that occurrence. It's a potent possibility. It's a simple phrase: black, white, gray, and blink. The invitation is to use it.

So what happened when you had that disrupting thought? When you began to question Seeing With Heart? When you began to tell yourself that the writings were not actually channeled; that I spun this story to bring mystery and intrigue to this experience?

I went from seeing birds flying to fish swimming, from an open heart to closing down. It was my mind, not yours, that spun a story and actually got in the way.

What did that feel like?

Unsettling.

Where did you feel that?

In my chest.

This is inevitable when we see only through the eight notes. Our minds play games with us. It's when we think too much that we self-sabotage and go to "This sounds like some far-fetched story."

I see now how my self-sabotaging thinking creates fear.

How do you feel now?

My whole body has opened. My whole being has softened.

What did you do?

I blinked. It feels empowering to have this choice.

walk straight into the mystery

Walk straight into the mystery in all of its majesty
and fully embrace that which frightens you the most.

Surrender. Let go.

Disregard the expectations of others
(the voices that attempt to bleed your soul)
by offering an unbounded outwardly flowing stream
of unconditional loving kindness.

In your heart, know that the universe always shows up perfectly,
reminding you that some of your most important nourishment
will come from that which tastes awful.

Openly embrace change, as it is not only inevitable – it is life,
providing us the opportunity to see beyond
the limited abilities of our ordinary eyes;
to see that for our spirits to be at peace, they must be at home.

Letting go is the way home, the way back into the stillness.
The place where the miracle is the ordinary not the exceptional.

The place of bliss.

What about the possibility of having the courage to **fully embrace that which frightens you the most?** What about having the authentic power, the authentic voice, to embrace that which is frightening? The power to surrender? To let go?

What about having the capacity to **disregard the expectations of others?** That's not about being selfish; that's about taking care of self. What about the possibility to *be* love when others judge us deeply; to be that **outwardly flowing stream of unconditional loving kindness?**

What about knowing that **our most important nourishment will come from that which tastes awful?** The invitation is to see that there is something relevant about each occurrence in our lives, no matter the flavor; to know that the only thing certain is uncertainty; that change is not only inevitable, it is simply life. Some days are sunny. Later in the day it's cloudy. Some days are cold. Others are hot. That's what they are.

What about having the capacity to let go and be in stillness even when it doesn't taste as we prefer? To be present with what is occurring, because that's life?

When we are present with what is occurring, and not judging, we flow abundance. However, when we perceive and judge abundance as exceptional, and identify it as a miracle, it stops. In fact, in most cases, miracles present as brief occurrences. Why? Because even the action of judging something remarkable interrupts the remarkable from continuing. When we stop judging, **the miracle is the ordinary not the exceptional.** It's our natural way of being.

These words speak deeply to what I feel. They remind me of so many situations throughout my life when I struggled but knew that I didn't have to. I didn't know what to do. I never learned how to make my way through those challenging situations. I am beginning to see how to shift my fear.

We are already seeing the potent medicine in the Seeing With Heart writings stir a remembrance of that which we already know; that which feels familiar. We are noticing that Seeing With Heart does not tell us what to do; it invites us to see how we feel. Does Seeing With Heart feel like that really comfortable, worn garment that you have been wearing for years that you would never throw away? Or does it feel like a foreign article of clothing that feels really stiff and constricting?

Definitely the comfortable, worn garment!

And what about the invitation to see with other than our ordinary eyes – the possibility to see and hear and taste and smell and touch all of the notes being played by all of the instruments in the orchestra, not just the eight notes? The point is that there is a much broader bandwidth, and Seeing With Heart speaks to that profoundly.

I sense that. I am beginning to see that. Even though I have tried to shift many times before, this time feels different. I already feel the shift occurring.

As we go along on the journey, Seeing With Heart invites us to use building blocks in a way that creates a light, stable framework. Using a chair as an example, we all know that when we build a chair with two legs it will fall over, and that a four-legged chair is stable. However, as we go about our lives we often build "forty-four-legged chairs" – we build protective structures around ourselves, become paralyzed, and are unable to respond. Does that sound familiar?

Yes. Very!

And for a chair to be stable, let's consider whether it even needs four legs.

No, three. A stool.

Right. And that's what Seeing With Heart does. It invites us to assemble a three-legged chair – a stool. It invites us to assemble a stable framework using the fewest number of building blocks so that we don't become paralyzed and are able to respond with grace and ease.

I like that. I really do. It works. I feel lighter already.

Paradigmatic Shift

You hear an invitation to begin journaling. As you listen closely, you realize that it is your voice, a feeling in your chest and in your belly. Take notice. Invite yourself to follow this calling. It is your medicine.

Gently encourage yourself to set time aside each day for journaling. Invite yourself to include challenging personal stories, exceptional situations, life-identifying moments, and even a letter to yourself. As your journal emerges, include experiences from early life memories to recent occurrences, from places of deep, loving connection to moments of "coincidence." No matter the flavor, invite yourself to share openly from your heart, for as you do you will begin to see patterns. Seeing With Heart invites you to explore these patterns and begin to see more clearly the common threads you weave through what appear to be distinctly different stories.

Is there anything you feel to share?

Yes. I feel that my journey is to heal wounds and brokenness that occurred when I was a child. I have recently been thinking about the similarity between how I was treated by my dad and how I have been treated by my boyfriends. I was looking at how I feel powerless and unable to express myself from my heart and feel safe. It's interesting to recognize how similar I am now to when I was little.

My dad was very domineering. He projected his anger by hitting, yelling, and criticizing me. I survived by pulling in. I didn't feel safe expressing myself. It wasn't until I began journaling that I realized how frequently I find myself in similar relationships. I feel like I'm doing the same thing over and over again, and already Seeing With Heart is helping me see this pattern. I'm seeking to heal and break this cycle so I can live fully from my heart. At times I feel like a little chick pecking at the eggshell and my little beak is starting to come out.

from afar

From afar,
a child calls,
from behind the breeze and before the waves.

Listen, for it is truth.

That's what these words speak to – the little chick pecking.

And also the little child.

Yes. **From afar, a child calls** – that's our inner voice, and **from behind the breeze** – our breath, and **before the waves** – our heartbeat. These words speak to that core place that resides within each of us – our very essence. **Listen, for it is truth.** Seeing With Heart invites us to listen to that "pecking." For when there is no pecking, we stay paralyzed – a wounded little child.

> *When you refer to being paralyzed, it reminds me of what I would do in that situation with my dad. I would freeze. To a certain degree I am still numb. Wow, I get it. All I need to do is keep pecking. It's kind of like the "blink" part of "black, white, grey, and blink."*

Yes. Even though the situation with your dad was not particularly the flavor you would have preferred, rather than being paralyzed for the rest of your life, the possibility exists to embrace Dad as an illuminating beacon in the fog – a potent opportunity for shift.

I am excited to embrace this possibility.

So when we are small and they are tall, we adapt to our situations in the only ways we know. In yours, you became numb. When we are numb, we are frozen, so we perpetuate those patterns, and the unhealthy cycle continues.

Yes. I've been living in this way.

And something I hear is that the predominant pattern for navigating life is banging our heads against the stone walls of our lives. (I actually bang my head against the wall repeatedly, very strongly!) How do you imagine this feels?

Excruciating. I am still banging my head, even in my current relationship. It's crazy. I'm so numb that I don't realize I am doing this!

When we repeatedly bang our heads against the wall, the sheetrock eventually starts to crumble. After years of this way of being, we eventually get into the other room, deeply bruising ourselves along the way. And there is only so much banging our bodies can take before they fall apart. It's no wonder that many of us live on medications for depression, insomnia, indigestion, heartburn, and ulcers. We are literally thinking ourselves crazy and eating ourselves up. The possibility exists to step to the side, look immediately adjacent to the wall where we've been banging our heads, and walk down the corridor. What about the word *corridor*? Cor-ridor?

Hmmm.

In Latin, *cor* means heart. Rather than going through the experiences of our lives having dense stone walls affecting our movements, the invitation is to step aside and move along the "cor-ridor" of the heart. And how we navigate that corridor, specifically how we flow love, precisely affects every occurrence. This point will become clear as we proceed further along. For now it is a reminder to choose love as the way to move, always. May I gently touch your shirt-sleeve?

Okay.

Prior to my jiggling your sleeve, did you have an awareness of the fabric touching your skin?

No.

When I touch a point on your clothing it brings your awareness to something that your body had filtered. Science calls that *jiggling* a noxious stimulus. So I ask you this question: What's Dad?

A noxious stimulus. (Chuckle.)

Yes. The invitation is to see that Dad is a tug on your shirt-sleeve to bring awareness to that piece of yourself that has been filtered – that piece calling out to heal. What does that mean? Let's consider that when we are born, each of us embodies as a unique soul. Our souls, although perfect, each have an "assignment" to heal. So the possibility is to see that all of our life experiences are combinations of gentle tugs and not-so-gentle tugs on our shirt-sleeves, illuminating our assignments. Until we complete those assignments, we repeat them. Sound familiar?

Yes. There are so many situations I can think of that fit this explanation. I am beginning to see what you mean about seeing the patterns in what appears to be patternless.

And when we're small and they're tall, we haven't developed the skills to take care of ourselves based on those tugs on our shirt-sleeves – those noxious stimuli. At times we even get our heads banged against the wall, literally. Your situation was to that extent. Many get it verbally.

I would say I got both.

So rather than saying "I grew up with a dad who abused me" or "Why do I always find myself in unhealthy relationships?" what about the possibility that there is another way to interpret these occurrences?

through the illusion

Through the illusion
of physical experience,

Soul speaks directly
to the splintered
piece of peace.

Read that again.

Through the illusion of physical experience – through Dad, your current relationship, and each and every one of your life experiences – **Soul speaks directly to the splintered piece of peace.** (Spelling out loud "P-I-E-C-E of P-E-A-C-E.")

Hmmm.

What is common about what happened when you were younger and what is happening now? Might it be that each offers an invitation to blink and shift your perception to heal the splintered piece of peace? Seeing With Heart invites us to consider that there are messages in each of our life occurrences even, and especially when, they feel overwhelming and taste awful.

The possibility is to blink, to resonate "from within without," to let go, to listen to the child calling, to step aside ever so slightly and gracefully walk down the corridor, flowing love rather than holding on to the wounded places that paralyze us from fully experiencing **the place where the miracle is the ordinary** [Session One].

When we blink we see birds flying through the light air rather than fish swimming through the dark water. We instantly shift without going anywhere. Blink happens like that. Once we wrap our hearts around this way of seeing, the charge – the visceral feeling often associated with the paralyzing experience – lessens.

When you were small and Dad was tall, the possibility was to see that those extremely challenging occurrences were actually your soul tugging at your shirt-sleeve saying, "This is about you. It is about the splintered piece of peace you embody. And until you fully go through that which you need to go through, you will continue to experience challenges, which are actually invisible blessings." Then suddenly, in a blink, you whisper, "Thank you, Dad."

And here you are many years later repeating the pattern. We are not going to be talking about this many years from now. We won't even be talking about this a few months from now.

It's crazy how I have been living. I don't want to do this anymore. I won't do this anymore!

That's right, you won't.

I'm already beginning to feel a softening.

That softening is the love you embody – your very essence. As we continue along, that softening will become more and more apparent.

I know it is here (pointing to self). I just forget. I know it is me.

We all forget. And what is happening now, through our individual and collective life occurrences, is that more than ever before we are remembering. We are waking up.

At times the experience of waking up can be very painful, even excruciating. As we expand the bandwidth, Seeing With Heart invites us to consider that the truth may actually contradict what we consider to be the truth. We might even come to see that what we desperately want to be true is in fact what is causing the excruciating pain. The invitation is to see that life is not about what we want; it's about what is. Just because we don't hear it, doesn't mean it isn't. Just because we don't see it, doesn't mean it's not. When we perceive through the eight notes – the narrow bandwidth – we don't hear the dog whistle or see the high-water mark. Rather than predetermining that the narrow bandwidth is reality, let's consider the possibility that there is a much broader bandwidth – a much broader reality.

And for some, the broader reality includes stories about "Dad." And those stories can stir deep emotions and even visceral responses. Like any journey, sometimes the Seeing With Heart terrain is challenging. It might even feel impassible – at times it even feels like the path narrowed and on one side there is a vertical stone wall while on the other there is a vertical drop-off. The invitation is to have the courage to walk that "impassible" portion of the terrain and continue along the journey. For invariably when we do, we reach destinations that far exceed what we considered possible.

Seeing With Heart isn't about leaving your life; it's about the possibility of gracefully integrating a new way of being into your life. It isn't about moving perpendicularly to your life or changing your core beliefs; it's about stepping aside ever so slightly and shifting to travel along on a parallel path in a parallel universe – a universe that fully supports the authentic expression of your very essence.

It's comfortable to know that Seeing With Heart is going to compliment my core beliefs. Knowing this makes me feel like I'm that little chick, pecking at the eggshell, about to break through.

there is a place

There is a place within each soul
from which the passion stirs the calling,
where the fire drips its luminescence,
birthing the dream place,
the sacred space in time
from which the passion comes to be.

There is a place within each soul from which the passion stirs the calling – a place that resides within each of us, **where the fire drips its luminescence, birthing the dream place, the sacred space in time from which the passion comes to be.** It's that little chick pecking from within. You can't see it through your ordinary eyes. You don't actually see it at all; you "see" it by feeling it. That's how you hear it as well. You are shifting to that way of seeing – the way of Seeing With Heart.

The more you listen closely to the tuggings on your shirt-sleeve, the more you wake up and remember that which makes you uniquely you, and me uniquely me. Do you remember when you were young and got caught looking out the window daydreaming during school? "Johnny, what's the answer to that math question?" "Uh, what math question?" Do you remember breaking out in a clammy sweat? "Johnny, you're not paying attention" – as if what you were doing was worthless. You were shamed and ridiculed for listening to that inner voice.

Hmmm. I am beginning to realize that I have been burying my dreams.

Early in our lives we learned to hide them in the deep recesses of our hearts. The invitation is to listen closely to our dreams, feel the tugs on our shirt-sleeves, and have the courage to shift from banging our heads against the stone walls of our lives.

Wow. I feel these words speak directly to me. I am seeing more clearly what I have been doing and, more important, what I have not been doing. It's like you have been saying: It's not about something Seeing With Heart is going to give me; it's about opening up to what I already am.

To Journey from Within

shhh, i hear a knocking

Shhh, I hear a knocking
from a distant place behind my heart.

Listen – a knocking.
Welcome, come in, I offer with outstretched arms.

As I open my heart I sense
the ethereal movement of joy
welling up as tears of love.

Initially, only vaguely familiar
(from that very distant place).

Then, with imperceptible movement
becoming more present until
finally, uncontainably, flowing over
and passionately caressing
the place where light becomes form.

What, I ask, is this knocking?

Oh, it is me.

With a gentle exhale, let the medicine in these words wash over us as a compassionate reminder that it is about opening up to what we already are.

Shhh, I hear a knocking. At first we hear something **from a distant place,** from deep within our hearts. Then, **Listen – a knocking. Welcome, come in, I offer with outstretched arms** is a call to not only hear but listen closely to and honor that core **piece of peace [Session Two]** that is you.

As I open my heart I sense the ethereal movement of joy welling up as tears of love. This calling speaks to how we flow love. It's about fully opening our hearts like the tenderness of two lovers softly gazing into each other's eyes. It is something we all know, as the most universal experience is the expression of love.

Initially, only vaguely familiar (from that very distant place). With these words Seeing With Heart invites us to ask ourselves why the love we flow is only vaguely familiar? Why does it feel to be flowing **from that very distant place?**

Because I have not been listening to my inner voice. "Vaguely familiar from that very distant place" reminds me of when I felt like a little chick pecking at the eggshell and my little beak was starting to come out.

Then, with imperceptible movement becoming more present. Initially we don't sense the movement within ourselves. Then as we open up to this way of seeing, the calling becomes more present, like a beacon in the fog. When we listen closely to this calling, we see the invisible threads connecting what appear to be distinctly separate occurrences in both our individual and collective lives. Seeing With Heart invites us to blink and embrace these invisible threads as relevant connections between each of our life occurrences. For as we do, we experience an expanding flow of abundance **until finally, uncontainably flowing over** – *flowing over* rather than *overflowing*. Picture an exquisite fountain flowing over rather than a bathtub overflowing.

The opening line – "There are no accidents" – in *Me, Finally* invites us to consider that there are no accidents; no coincidences; no random, discrete events. What about the possibility that the accidents; coincidences; and random, discrete events of our lives are actually the invisible threads connecting us all as one? Who is it that is calling you to read these words, to listen closely? Is it me? No. It is you. It is the feeling you have to listen closely. And where do you feel this calling to listen?

In my heart. In fact, I feel it right now as we are talking. I have been feeling it for quite a while. I was afraid to listen. I feel that I no longer have an option to be afraid. I must listen.

What do the words **passionately caressing the place where light becomes form** invite us to consider? Let's separate them into two phrases. **The place where light becomes form** speaks to the place within each of us where our soul – our very essence – becomes self. **Passionately caressing** is a gentle invitation to embrace that place with love. So where in our bodies do we feel these experiences?

In our hearts.

What, I ask, is this knocking? Oh, it is me.

That's so beautiful. It's simple. As I open my heart, I open up me! What a beautiful reminder to stop forgetting myself. I get it! These poems are guiding me on my own journey of healing.

embrace the possibility

Embrace the possibility
of not thinking about
anything,

expanding instead,

from within the place
of feeling about
everything.

These words invite us to navigate life by feeling our way. For when we do, we are always exactly and precisely where we need to be. And when we are thinking, we are never where we need to be. For example, let's consider what happens when you're struggling with whether to quit your job. When you think about what to do, the mind runs wild with the rhetorical dialogue of "should I or shouldn't I?" Instead, when you listen closely to what you are feeling, clarity emerges.

The invitation to make our way by "feeling not thinking" might feel counterintuitive. This is because we have overdeveloped our tendency to analyze rather than trusting our guts. This often leads to second-guessing and waffling on our decisions.

Of course thinking does provide support for navigating our logistical lives – those practical matters such as when to wake up to be on time for work. However, when it comes to navigating those occurrences that touch our hearts, thinking undermines our experiences of ease. In these areas of our lives we often make mountains out of molehills or molehills out of mountains. We do this all the time.

For example, the patient who presents saying, "I think I have a brain tumor." "Why would you think that?"

"Because I woke up today with a migraine." This is an example of the dis-ease we create when thinking our way to an answer. We make mountains out of molehills before we even know the facts. We create fear by "thinking ourselves crazy."

Far more serious is the patient who complains of a headache, and then on the way out of the office mentions that they have been passing blood in their urine for the past three days. "Oh, it will get better. It's no big deal." They are ignoring these symptoms even though they feel in their gut that something is wrong. This is an example of what happens when we make molehills out of mountains. This is what we do. We ignore the symptoms – the messages life offers – even though we feel that something needs attention. We get stuck in the thinking, neglect our feelings, and fail to trust our gut.

Wow. I really do think myself crazy and make mountains out of molehills. I'm not even sure how to know whether I'm thinking or feeling.

That's a great insight. Seeing With Heart invites us to use the visceral experience of how we are feeling to determine to what extent we are feeling compared to thinking. We all know what it feels like to experience ease in our chests and bellies. Likewise, when something is troubling, we know how unsettled those areas of our bodies feel. So it is actually very simple to differentiate. The extent to which we feel ease compared to feeling unsettled is a precise reflection of the extent to which we are feeling as opposed to thinking. When we think ourselves crazy, we create the unsettled feeling – the dis-ease. "Am I feeling not thinking?" – a simple question.

> *Wow, that's something I can easily do throughout the day. I can use "feeling not thinking" as a reminder to check in when I am feeling unsettled – those times that I am thinking myself crazy.*

so often we hide

So often we hide
behind "smile at the surface."

Only fooling ourselves,
through the fooling of others.

Rather, smiling from gut
calls the true smile of heart,
flowing out through the eyes,
the true smile of peace.

So often we hide behind "smile at the surface." This is the way we cover up the unsettled feelings, the dis-ease. It's what we do when we are predominantly thinking, not feeling.

I'm sad to say that I have lived that way. When I'm scared and miserable inside I use my smile as a shield. Somebody asks, "How are you doing?" and smiling I reply, "Fine, and you?" when actually I don't feel fine and I'm not being honest.

It's a reflex. And when we do that, we are **only fooling ourselves, through the fooling of others.** "I don't want to hurt somebody's feelings, so I'd better not speak up." We default to being doormats and making ourselves invisible.

That's what I've been doing throughout my entire life. I've been invisible. I am so insecure about myself that I actually avoid meeting people. I am afraid of someone asking, "What are you doing now?" because whatever I am doing is never good enough. So instead, I smile.

Yes, we do this. You are not alone. And it's only when we begin to see these unhealthy patterns that we can let them go. **Smiling from gut calls the true smile of heart** speaks to opening up in a way that allows us to navigate predominantly by "feeling not thinking" – living fearless lives of flowing over, not overflowing.

The invitation for each of us is to step out from behind the **smile at the surface,** from behind the fear and the being invisible, and have the courage to be **the true smile of peace.**

it is the yearning

It is the yearning that often drives us
further away from that from which we came.

We look outward
that's what the yearning does.

There must be something, someone, somebody,
any body, any thing, out there to fill the yearning,

kNOw,

it can only be filled by returning to self
by returning to the love from which we came.

The possibility is to see that **it is the yearning that often drives us further away from that from which we came.** When we see through the eight notes – the narrow bandwidth – we see our lives as collections of separate bits and pieces. Often these pieces are very alluring and lead us to the yearning. And what about the yearning? **We look outward; that's what the yearning does.** We believe **there must be something, someone, somebody, any body, any thing, out there to fill the yearning.** "My life will be great when I have the perfect job, the perfect partner, the perfect house."

I can see now that I often buy things to feel good. I also tend to make other people happy before I make myself happy.

59

I am beginning to see now how I have been perpetuating this pattern.

This is what happens when we look outside of ourselves – when we are seeking. Whether it's concerning ourselves with what another thinks of us or believing our peace and happiness will come from the things we need to own, **kNOw, it can only be filled by returning to self by returning to the love from which we came. NO,** (spelling N-O), **it can only be filled by returning to self. kNOw,** (spelling K-N-O-W), that **it can only be filled by returning to self by returning to the love from which we came** – by awakening the love of self.

I'm really seeing how important it is for me to look for peace and happiness from within.

it's not about the outside

It's not about the outside,
or even reaching to the in,
for to taste the peace of love,
sip the seeing from within.

It's not about the outside. As we are seeing, inner peace will not occur by seeking.

And what about **reaching to the in?** Although less obvious, this is yet another way of seeking, since we are still looking for something to fix. The possibility is to see that we already have peace. It is always there. **For to taste the peace of love, sip the seeing from within.** What about the last two words of this phrase: **from within?** With these words Seeing With Heart invites us to consider that inner peace is not about looking out, nor is it about looking in; it's about the possibility of embracing our lives **from within.**

Earlier we shared the words **flowing over at the place where light becomes form [Session Three].** There's something relevant about that flowing over. We know that all of life is comprised of moving energy. So rather than looking at energy as something outside of ourselves, and rather than looking at it as something that is flowing in, the possibility is to see energy as something that is flowing out **from within.**

This point invites us to blink once again and shift our perceptions. The potent possibility is to see our lives as responses to how we are *flowing over* from within rather than as consequences of all of the separate bits and pieces

61

that appear to be random, discrete events; to journey *from within* the cor-ridors of our hearts, our souls. Then we know that inner peace is not about needing to find peace in our lives; it's about cultivating that which we already have.

Flow from Within

Before we continue on our way, let's pause to check in and see if there is anything you feel to share from your journaling?

> *It's funny that you ask about journaling. Having never journaled before, I am finding that setting time aside for writing has been healing for me. May I read something I wrote last night?*

Please do.

> *"I feel amazed. So much has occurred so quickly. It's remarkable. I blink and rather than seeing fish swimming, I see birds flying. Rather than looking outside of myself, I truly see that I am flowing from within. From this awareness I feel a profound shift in my body, an inner strength, an inner calm."*

Have you ever experienced this before?

> *No, I haven't. It's profound.*

What might be shifting for this to have occurred?

I clearly feel myself moving from my head into my body, from thinking to feeling. For the first time in my life I am feeling from my heart, flowing from within.

What are you noticing that's different when you are "being" in this way?

I am noticing a greater sense of calm. In the past I typically made mountains out of molehills, which often resulted in chaos. Now when I find myself in unsettling experiences, I blink. I actually blink and recognize the moment before something escalates as a tug on my shirt-sleeve.

How does that feel?

Remarkable! So often those types of situations would have spiraled into something I would end up regretting. Now I find myself embracing them as opportunities.

This is what I hear from so many who have made this journey. As we individually and collectively embody the possibility that we really are flowing from within, we shift quickly.

eyes that taste the texture

With eyes that taste the texture,
look beyond the ordinary.

Expand from within the oneness,
from within the streaming fluid energy
flowing out from and in through
the illusion of the me and the you.

Walk straight into this seeing,
fully tasting this texture,
the texture of the tapestry of one.

With eyes that taste the texture, look beyond the ordinary. These words speak directly to a way of being that doesn't limit the experience of taste to our mouths. When we are seeing with other than our ordinary eyes, the definite boundaries we so readily accept as reality dissolve, inviting us to **expand from within the oneness.**

As we embrace this way of being, we expand the bandwidth and see **the streaming fluid energy flowing out from and in through the illusion of the me and the you.** The word *illusion* invites us to see that behind the compartments of our senses there is a unified field of energy flowing from within. When we invite ourselves to this way of seeing, we have direct experiences with this unified field. We awaken to knowing that what we see through our ordinary eyes are precise reflections of how the energy is **flowing out from and in through the illusion of the me and the you.**

The invitation is to **walk straight into this seeing, fully tasting this texture, the texture of the tapestry of one.** For when we do, rather than seeing our day-to-day experiences solely through the lens of the "me" and the "you" – through only the eight notes – we see the physical experiences in our lives as potent messages illuminating our way to heal.

> *Although we've only been on this journey for a short while, I'm already beginning to see my life experiences in this way. I have an exciting story to share with you! For some time I've struggled to communicate with a co-worker. Our interactions are typically uncomfortable and often lead to knots in my stomach. Because of Seeing With Heart, I let go of the drama we have been creating. Earlier today I walked into her office, expressed my gratitude for her support, and gave her a hug. Now I see how my relationship with her is actually a message for me to heal from within.*

It's amazing that you have already experienced such a powerful shift!

It really is!

from deep within the mystery

From deep within the mystery,
somewhere just behind the place of separation,
the illumination of pure love pours out through the heart.

It is here, in this place where the unmanifest begins its journey to form,
that pure love shifts to desire.

This shift is the very foundation of the illusion of separation,
for as desire is drawn out from the heart it slowly infuses the senses
triggering the alluring call from the mind.

The call to the over-wanting and over-needing.

Resist this call with balanced intention, and embrace desire as pure love
by making strong the love of self.

Moving back to the somewhere just behind the place of separation,
where the love of heart leads us from within,
intimately connecting us to all
as one.

From deep within the mystery. What is the mystery? It's that sacred place within each of us, our divine essence, our soul. Seeing With Heart invites us to see the mystery as flowing from **somewhere just behind the place of separation,** from just ever-so-slightly behind our beating hearts.

It is from this mystery – our soul – that **the illumination of pure love pours out through the heart.** The potential to flow with pure love – unconditional love – resides within each of us. And how pure love flows out through our hearts precisely determines our individual and collective physical experiences.

It is here, in this place where the unmanifest begins its journey to form, that pure love shifts to desire. This speaks to the shift that occurs as pure love flows out through the heart, where light becomes form, where love becomes the illusion of the me and the you. Seeing With Heart invites us to see that our lives unfold as a fluctuating stream of experiences. These experiences precisely reflect the extent of pure love – the amount of acceptance in relationship to judgment that we flow from within. We love. We hate. We play. We struggle. We flow all of this through the illusion of the me and the you.

Let's circle back to revisit the image of the cor-ridor, the conduit through which we flow love. Rather than seeing the corridor as having a static width, Seeing With Heart invites us to see the corridor as a fluctuating aperture, an aperture that literally changes diameter depending on how we are flowing love from within.

Are you familiar with photography?

Not really.

Okay. To illustrate this point, cameras have mechanisms called shutters that open or close an aperture. The setting of this aperture precisely determines how much light flows through the lens. This metaphor relates to how we flow "light through our lens" – how we flow love through our "cor-ri-doors," our "heart doors."

Oh, right. (In a soft, whispering voice of realization.)

Seeing With Heart is inviting us to consider that our physical experiences are precise reflections of how we fluctuate our apertures. To the extent that we flow unconditional love in relationship to conditional love – the love of acceptance in relationship to the love of judgment, the aperture fluctuates. For example, when you say, "I am not good enough," what does the aperture look like?

Very, very tiny. I'm picturing a pinhole.

What does it feel like when you are being in this way?

It feels really tight and constricted in my chest.

Right. So the possibility is to embrace the awareness that we each embody a fluctuating aperture. And it is our *soul purpose* to expand that aperture by using the "ordinary" experiences of our lives as illuminating beacons.

To further illustrate this point, picture a purse that closes by pulling its strings outward in opposite directions. We have an option to pull the strings, closing the purse shut and constricting our flow of love, or to release the strings, opening the purse wide and expanding abundantly the flow of love from within.

This shift is the very foundation of the illusion of separation. To the extent that pure love shifts to desire – to the extent that the love of acceptance shifts to the love of expectation, we manifest separation. For example, in a practical, real-life sense, the more we judge each other, the more we separate. When you tell me that I should do this and I tell you that you should do that, we flow through the pinhole and experience dis-ease – that familiar feeling of tightness in our chests.

And from the deeper purpose of our divine essence, Seeing With Heart invites us to consider that the aperture we each embody is precisely reflected through the illusion of separation – the illusion of the me and the you. Our aperture is the embodiment of our spiritual assignment – our spiritual calling to heal.

Something I hear is that our assignments are not readily apparent. In fact they are essentially invisible, **for as desire is drawn out from the heart it slowly infuses the senses, triggering the alluring call from the mind.** We see. We hear. We taste. We smell. We touch. Because we are wired to see through our five senses – the eight notes – we don't even realize that our life occurrences are actually the tugs on our shirt-sleeves.

Are you suggesting that the way we perceive through our five senses is related to the tugs on our shirt-sleeves?

Yes. When we perceive our life experiences only through our five senses, we limit our perception to the narrow bandwidth and see each experience as an occurrence that is unrelated to anything other than itself. When we expand the bandwidth, we see the tugs on our shirt-sleeves. We see that every bit and piece, every one of our life experiences, is actually an opportunity to heal the **splintered piece of peace [Session Two].** We see the medicine that is occurring in all of us.

The call to the over-wanting and over-needing. I see something. I want it. I see something. I need it. **Resist this call with balanced intention, and embrace desire as pure love by making strong the love of self.**

The love of self?

Yes. Seeing With Heart is asking us to look at the importance of self-acceptance and self-care – the love of self.

Moving back to the somewhere just behind the place of separation, where the love of heart leads us from within, intimately connecting us to all as one. To the extent that we flow with acceptance, without expectation of others and especially with ourselves, we flow ripples of loving compassion intimately connecting us all as one.

Wow. This is remarkable. I'm really seeing that my experience of love and inner peace is not only about flowing from within; it's about how I'm flowing from within.

Yes. So let's paint another picture. This time let's look at the Hoover Dam. For all intents and purposes there is an infinite amount of water behind the dam – an infinite amount of love behind our hearts.

Now let's envision using a theoretical tool to pierce a very fine hole through the wall, a pinhole. Even though there is an "infinite" amount of water behind it, because of the extremely small diameter of the hole, the water only trickles out, dribbling down the face of the wall.

This is what we do in our lives. So often our apertures are pinholes. I'm sure we can relate to those occasions when we are dribbling on ourselves. That's what we do when we flow *conditional* love – love burdened with judgment and expectation. Sound familiar?

Yes. So many examples that have occurred over the years come to my awareness.

Is there one you feel to share about?

Yes, Dad. Even though we have had a very challenging relationship, I know he loves me. He just doesn't love himself.

Actually he does, but with a deep, conditional love of self. What you were seeing when you were small and he was tall was Dad's "dribbling" projection of self-judgment.

Right. I really see that now.

So as we continue to enlarge the diameter of the hole – opening our aperture, the flow of water shifts from trickling down the wall – from dribbling on ourselves – to an increasingly powerful stream of water flowing – an increasingly powerful stream of unconditional love flowing from within. Then, with only a small additional increase in the diameter of the hole proportionate to the entire size of the wall, there comes a point when the power contained in the water literally blows the wall open. The concrete and all of the internal structures used to reinforce the wall instantly let go. That's blink;

that's about our apertures instantly opening wide, instantly expanding our flow of unconditional love. That's about our hearts opening in a way that to this point we might not have even dreamed possible.

What a remarkable picture. I see that I've been opening my aperture little by little. I see that it doesn't take much. A gentle shift, and very powerful changes are occurring.

Yes. The potent medicine of Seeing With Heart accelerates this shift. What we are looking at is the difference between continuing to bang our heads against the stone walls of our lives, and gently stepping aside and walking down the cor-ridors – walking down our true heart paths. That's the difference between a linear curve and an exponential curve, the difference between 1 - 2 - 3 - 4 - 5 - 6 and 1 - 2 - 4 - 8 - 16 - 32 - 64. It's a potent possibility. It's a paradigmatic shift.

I've been doing this and I didn't even know that I've been doing this. I am actually seeing pieces of my life that I have struggled with for years literally changing within days.

And to the extent that we "be" this way, unconditional love flows with increasing ease from ever-so-slightly behind the walls of our Hoover Dams – from ever-so-slightly behind our beating hearts.

I feel an incredible spaciousness in my chest. It's precious.

SESSION FIVE

Illusion of Separation

This morning something intriguing occurred that I feel to share.

Okay.

As I was preparing for the day, I realized that I had slept in the socks I wore yesterday. Then I had a thought: "I don't want you to see me in the same socks." I went right to being self-conscious and judgmental. Instantly I realized I had closed my aperture. I actually felt the constriction in my chest. Then something profound occurred. I blinked, effortlessly shifting back to "feeling not thinking." I felt the constriction in my chest soften. I felt the aperture open. I decided not to change my socks. I decided not to worry about what you think of me. I completely let go of being self-conscious and of judging myself.

Do you want to hear a secret? I'm wearing the same socks as yesterday.

I noticed that.

(Laughing together.)

This is a perfect example of how we make mountains out of molehills. When we are "seeing with head" we get caught in our thinking ways. We self-sabotage and undermine our abilities to navigate clearly what we are truly feeling. Why would it matter what I think about your socks?

It really doesn't. It feels good to do what I feel and not fear being judged. It's really amazing to know that I have the inner strength to navigate my life with greater ease — to navigate with an open heart. I'm feeling to share something I wrote last night when journaling.

Okay.

"As I reflect back to the beginning of our Seeing With Heart journey, when we paused to focus on nothing other than our breath, I remember feeling a deep inner peace. I am now realizing that that experience was actually the result of opening my aperture, opening my heart."

It's profound to know that we have the capacity to fluctuate that flow; that it's not being regulated for us by something outside of ourselves.

Yes. That reminds me of an experience I had five years ago. I was invited to a friend's house for chanting and meditation. While I was chanting I saw a heart surrounded by fire. I started to cry. Afterward my friend said that that was the guru flowing energy into me.

Interesting. How would you speak to that now after what we've shared?

At the time I believed her that it was something greater than me; that it was the power of the guru that brought the vision and the tears. Now I know that I flowed that experience from within; that it was a precise reflection of my aperture. For the first time I am seeing that what I do with the aperture actually occurs.

So what were those tears?

Love. The tears were love flowing out from within. I remember how I felt at that moment. I had never felt like that before. My whole being was completely full of love. Now I actually see that it was me flowing through my heart. It was me opening up to me. I'm the guru.

Exactly! As we had mentioned earlier in the journey, Seeing With Heart invites us to see that the only guru is the guru from within. Seeing With Heart is effective because it's not me teaching you my way; it's you making your way. And when we make our ways by kicking dirt, we make dust storms. When we say we can't, we won't. In fact, there is actually a different feeling when we say the word *can't* compared to when we say the word *can* – an entirely different vibrational resonance. When we say we *can't*, what do we create in our lives?

Nothing.

What happens to our aperture?

It pinches tight.

Yes. Paralysis. The invitation is to see that everything we do and everything we say affects the vibrational resonance of the ripples we flow from within.

That is so potent, so powerful.

And yet we are so quick to give that power away. So often we give it to that which is outside of ourselves – the shopping mall, the job title, the size of our homes, the guru. Even in our own spiritual pursuits we predominantly follow someone else's way rather than flowing our own way.

To the extent in our daily lives that we stop saying "can't," and blink, our apertures open wide and in that instant we recognize that we are the gurus. It is a paradigmatic shift, instantaneously moving away from perpetuating our old ways of being and fully stepping into our natural ways of being.

As we experience this paradigmatic shift, we see, hear, taste, smell, and touch all of the eighty-eight notes on the piano. We see the broader bandwidth. As we do, we see the patterns in what appears to be patternless. We see why the water moves farther up the shoreline when the moon is full. We see that *it's never about what it's about.* We see the invisible threads connecting us all as one.

an eyelash

An eyelash
resting just a moment above the horizon,
flings out its glitter upon the blackness.

As this fairy dust dances,
the enchanted ocean comes alive,
radiant with luminescent iridescence.

All the while,
the crescent moonrise tugs
at our very cores,
with its invisible strings,
moving our naked souls
as magic marionettes.

Ah, the majesty of miracle.

An eyelash represents the visible threads, that which we see through our ordinary eyes, the me and the you, the continual stream of what appear to be entirely unrelated occurrences.

Resting just a moment above the horizon speaks to an awareness that is emerging from within each of us. This awareness **flings out its glitter upon the blackness;** it illuminates a way of seeing that as of yet we have not seen.

As this fairy dust dances, as we awaken to this awareness, **the enchanted ocean comes alive, radiant with luminescent iridescence.** So does the infinity of potential that resides within each of us.

All the while, the crescent moonrise tugs at our very cores, with its invisible strings, moving our naked souls as magic marionettes. In our daily lives we experience continual streams of what often appear to be entirely unrelated occurrences. The invitation is to see these occurrences as invisible threads tugging at our very cores — as potent messages that literally move us through our lives.

As mentioned earlier in our journey, the possibility is to see that all of our life experiences are combinations of gentle tugs and not-so-gentle tugs on our shirt-sleeves, illuminating our assignments. Until we complete those assignments, we repeat them.

The invisible threads are the interconnectedness of the tugs on our individual and collective shirt-sleeves. From this perspective we expand our bandwidths, seeing that even though our lives are comprised of continual streams of discernibly different events, there are actually patterns in what appears to be patternless. We see that there are no coincidences; there are no random, discrete events; there simply are no accidents.

Hearing you share about this way of interpreting our lives makes so much sense. Before beginning the Seeing With Heart journey, I only ever saw my life from the perspective of basically good experiences and bad experiences. Now I am seeing the relationship between the invisible threads and the fluctuating aperture.

Yes, the invisible threads are actually precise reflections of our fluctuating apertures.

Right! So when I hold on to Dad and past occurrences that were steeped in drama, the aperture remains constricted and I continue to manifest those "Dad" situations through my co-worker. Then I express gratitude to my co-worker, expanding the aperture, and my relationship with Dad improves significantly. I'm really seeing the patterns in what appears to be patternless — that there really are no random, discrete events. I'm really seeing what happens as I actually fluctuate my aperture.

Ah, the majesty of miracle. As we step fully into this way of seeing, we each see *me, finally*. What about the phrase *me, finally?* What does it mean to you?

It's about taking care of myself. It's about getting to know me. For as long as I can remember I've never felt confident. It goes all the way back to those painful situations with my dad. I would literally freeze and disappear. I wasn't good enough. I wasn't pretty. I wasn't going to amount to anything. I can think of so many situations throughout my life when I did this. In fact, I'm now seeing that it is this uncomfortable piece about myself that's at the core of what brought me to make this journey with you.

Would you elaborate?

Prior to Seeing With Heart my pattern was to stay busy and fill my days with distraction. My life was an emotional roller coaster with intervals of happiness. I realize now that I was actually running from myself. Wow, it's amazing that I'm saying this; that I'm seeing this now so clearly.

Why do you feel you are?

Because I am really clear about what happens as I fluctuate my aperture. I realize that for all these years my aperture has essentially been a pinhole and that my flow of love has been very restricted. I am now seeing that to this point I really haven't known myself; I haven't been me at all!

It seems that you are feeling differently now.

Definitely. Now I see that it's not difficult to be me. I open my aperture and I be me, finally.

What does that feel like?

Spacious. Serene. Empowering. I find that I'm responding differently to situations that in the past would have gotten me all pinched up. I feel like I have an infinite amount of love that's emerging.

tell me everything

"Tell me everything,"
uttered the small child.

"Alright." (pause)
"There is only love.
That is everything,"
whispered the breeze.

Please read that again.

"Tell me everything," uttered the small child. This speaks to the infinite potential that resides within each of us. **"Alright." (pause) "There is only love. That is everything," whispered the breeze.** And that infinite potential that resides within each of us is love.

83

Okay, it sounds great to say that there is only love, but what about all those times in my life when bad things happened to me? What about all the hatred in the world? What about all the catastrophes?

Yes, it's true. At times we experience the bad, the hatred, and the catastrophes – those occurrences in our lives that taste painfully awful. What do you feel is occurring as we experience these extremes?

The aperture is fluctuating and affecting the flow of love.

Exactly. Notice that you didn't say the flow of bad things, the flow of hatred, the flow of catastrophes. Although we often see what looks like bad, hatred, and catastrophes, **"There is only love. That is everything," whispered the breeze.**

I get that we are flowing love, but if there is only love, why is there so much conflict in our world?

Seeing With Heart invites us to see that that which we see is a precise reflection of that which we be. When we kick dirt, we make dust storms. When we flow judgment, we see bad and hatred. And through the illusion of the me and the you – the illusion of "I'm right and you're wrong," we co-create catastrophe – even wars, acts of terrorism, and natural disasters.

This way of seeing our lives might feel raw and might not resonate with you. However, the invitation is for us to see that as we expand the bandwidth and see the invisible threads, we can see the interconnectedness in all that we see. We see that there are no random, discrete events; that our individual and collective experiences are precise reflections of that which we be.

So what you're saying is that the bad, hatred, and catastrophes are reflections of flowing love through extremely tight apertures?

Yes. The opportunity is for us to see that there is no bad, hatred, or catastrophe. There is only the appearance of these aspects of ourselves as reflections of pinhole apertures.

Remember earlier in our journey when Seeing With Heart invited us to **know that the universe always shows up perfectly, reminding us that some of our most important nourishment will come from that which tastes awful [Session One]?** The possibility is to know that there is potent medicine in all that we see, especially and particularly in that which tastes awful.

Would we not concur that it's during those times of conflict that strangers come together and support each other with the most beautiful expressions of love? Is it not during those times that we are the most selfless? Why? Because it is our true nature – our very essence. At our very cores, we are love.

As we embody this awareness, a subtle yet profound shift occurs. And rather than banging our heads against the bad, the hatred, and the catastrophes of our lives, we move ever so slightly to the side and flow with ease through our "cor-ri-doors," our "heart doors."

And I'm finding that it has only taken a subtle shift to be love.

It's interesting that you said "be love" rather than "being loving." We are often so intent on being loving that we forget to be love. It might seem like a subtle difference, however the energetic difference between those two phrases is significant.

Even though I said it that way, I'm not certain I understand the difference.

Being loving is about doing something for someone else – for something outside of ourselves. Although this appears to be the way we think we should be with one another, what occurs from this way of being is that we develop expectations and judgment. "I am being loving for you, so why are you not being loving for me?" "I help you with what you need to do, so why don't you help me with what I need to do?" Then we go quickly to "You must not love me." In this way we are basing our happiness on that which is outside of ourselves, and we are happy only when others respond the way we think they should. Rather, the invitation is to be love, open the aperture, and flow ripples of loving compassion. Seeing With Heart reminds us that that which we see is a precise reflection of that which we be. So the extent to which we be love is the extent to which we see love.

> *I see. As I open my pinhole aperture, I shift from being loving – from flowing love predominantly burdened with expectation, to be love – flowing love of acceptance. For example, when I walked into my co-worker's office, expressed my gratitude, and gave her a hug, not only did my relationship with her improve considerably, it's remarkable that I've even seen other relationships improve as well, including my relationship with Dad.*

That's right. And through the invisible threads – the ripples of love we flow from within – we weave a tapestry of the precise love that we be. So the invitation is to be love, because when Dad comes to his final breath and you are sitting alongside one another, will you say, "That was a really nice car you got me for my sixteenth birthday" or "That was a really nice couch you and Mom got for the house"? What will you say?

I love you.

Yes. Three words. I love you. That's all there is.

There is only love. (With tears flowing.)

Love of Self

everything begins with

Everything begins with loving the self,
yet we're so terribly afraid of "I love me."

We listen instead to the voice that's so haunting,
the one from so far away.

"Don't be so selfish, you must think of the others,
and don't hug yourself or spend time with your soul.
For remember there's nothing to show from these pleasures,
nothing productive, nothing to weigh."

"No!" cries your spirit.

"This is not about selfish, it's about the importance of caring for self.
And doing exactly what one needs in the moment,
by feeling with gut,
the feeling of true."

For being authentic with spirit and soul
is the one single choice that will move us to whole.

Only then can "I love me" and can "I love you"
as they're actually but one in the same.

Let's reflect on the potent medicine in these words.

Everything begins with loving the self, yet we're so terribly afraid of "I love me."

> *That's so true. I have been afraid to love myself. In fact, I frequently say "I love you," and to this point I've never even considered saying "I love me."*

It feels natural to say "I love you." Yet when looking in the mirror, it feels unnatural to speak that phrase to ourselves.

> *Why is that?*

Seeing With Heart invites us to see that **we listen instead to the voice that's so haunting, the one from so far away;** that rather than listening to our inner voice and doing what we *feel* to do, we predominantly do what we *think* we should do based on what others say we should do. That is why Seeing With Heart invites us to say "I feel to..." instead of "I think I should..."

> *Throughout my life I really did that. Now I find myself reaching into my heart pocket and pulling out the phrase "feeling not thinking." And when I do, I find that it doesn't matter what others say I should do.*

When we find the courage to follow our inner voices we often hear **"Don't be so selfish; you must think of the**

others. And don't hug yourself or spend time with your soul." Isn't it interesting that self-care and self-love are often confused with being self-absorbed and selfish?

Yes. I've often put others first. So instead of paying attention to my needs, my inner voice, I've been going about my days helping everyone else. It's always been hard for me to say no to others. Now I'm learning to honor myself and say Yes! to me.

What has shifted?

My aperture! It's so much more open. Seeing With Heart has been so helpful in providing tools for following my heart. This might seem silly but I even find myself taking time in the day to pause and hug myself. When I do, I feel happy and peaceful.

That's such a beautiful way of being. Yet others will say that **there's nothing to show from these pleasures, nothing productive, nothing to weigh.** So often we base our self-worth on whether there is something that can be measured, something tangible. We still find ourselves weighing in with the job title, the automobile we drive, or the logos we wear. To a large extent we've been basing our love of self on our success in the outside world.

"No!" cries your spirit. More than ever before many are hearing the potent medicine of hugging yourself and spending time with your soul. Many are literally waking up to this way of weighing in.

I used to place more importance on what other people thought I should do and how many items I accomplished on my to-do list. Now I know what is most important to me isn't necessarily something someone else will see at the end of the day.

And that's when we know **this is not about selfish, it's about the importance of caring for self.** For example, when you're flying with your children and the oxygen masks deploy, whose mask do you put on first?

My children's!

No, actually your own! Unless you care for yourself first you will never truly be able to care for another. How helpful will you be to your children when you lose consciousness while reaching to put their masks on? In fact, I imagine that in your heart you knew to put your mask on first. However, you are so accustomed to helping everyone else first that the knee-jerk response was "My children's."

That's right.

We go so quickly to that thinking place. Instead, the possibility is to follow your inner voice by **doing exactly what one needs in the moment, by feeling with gut, the** feeling of true. For being authentic with spirit and soul is the one single choice that will move us to whole. So the invitation for each of us is to hold sacred the love of self.

Only then can "I love me" and can "I love you," as they're actually but one in the same. For when we are in this way of being, it's as natural to say "I love me" as it is to say "I love you."

> That's so beautiful. Now I see that throughout my life I've struggled with loving myself. I felt that to be really loving I had to help everyone else first. And yet when I did, I often felt unsettled.

Do you know why you felt that way?

> I am beginning to understand that no matter how much I would do and do and do, I would feel that I needed to do more and more and more to be loved.

Yes. The unsettled feeling is actually coming from the always doing for others. It's a tug on the shirt-sleeve, precisely illuminating the fluctuating aperture – the love of self. When you're feeling unsettled, what's happening with your aperture?

> It's pinched down. I can't do that anymore. I won't do that anymore.

why do we find ourselves

But why do we find ourselves
in unwanted places?

Those situations we prefer
to not really be in.

It's all about boundaries and caring for self,
in the love that transcends the illusion of me.

These patterns of being
speak directly to core;
the core of our soul that screams out to be,
in all of its splendor and all of its beauty,
in the fullness of love,
with the all of the we.

But why do we find ourselves in unwanted places? Why is it that no matter how hard we try, we still end up in **those situations we prefer to not really be in?** Is it possible that there is something relevant about each and every one of those occurrences?

Earlier in our journey we spoke about there being no coincidences – that there are actually patterns in what appears to be patternless. Seeing With Heart invites us to see that although our lives appear to be comprised of random, discrete events, there are actually precise patterns to the unwanted places. And when we begin to see these patterns, we see there is potent medicine in **those situations we prefer to not really be in.**

Rather than feeling that yet another "bad" thing just happened, the possibility is to see the relationship between those situations and the fluctuating aperture – the love of self.

I'm not sure I understand.

How we fluctuate the aperture – how we flow love at the place where light becomes form, where love becomes the illusion of the "me" – actually regulates the situations we experience. When we kick dirt, we make dust storms. Likewise, to the extent that we judge ourselves – to the extent that we struggle with self-esteem and self-acceptance, we literally manifest unwanted places.

Are you saying that I create the unwanted places?

Yes. Rather than seeing those unwanted places as occurrences that are happening to you, the possibility is to see them manifesting as precise reflections of the love of self. And the love of self – "I love me" – precisely regulates the fluctuating aperture. In fact, the possibility is to see that the love of self and the fluctuating aperture are actually interchangeable. That's why "I love me" is so important. It's like home plate in the game of baseball. It's the place where we stand and "swing the bat." And as we develop our ability to swing the bat – as we develop our authentic love of self, the aperture fluctuates. When we invite ourselves to see this possibility, we see the patterns in what previously appeared to be patternless. We see the relevance of the unwanted places. Instead of being bad occurrences, we see them providing opportunities for clarity – illuminating beacons in the fogs of our lives.

So how do I stop creating the unwanted places?

It's all about boundaries and caring for self, in the love that transcends the illusion of me. There's potent medicine in seeing that we don't have to do and do and do; that we don't have to help everyone else first. The potent medicine is knowing the importance of caring for self. In fact, the more we individually and collectively hug ourselves, the more we flow ripples of loving compassion and the less we find ourselves in those unwanted places.

These patterns of being speak directly to core; the core of our soul that screams out to be, in all of its splendor and all of its beauty, in the fullness of love, with the all of the we. This way of being is the way of navigating from our very cores, our very essences. It is about listening closely to our inner voices – the voices that sing out to be the infinity of love that resides within each of us. And as we open our hearts and collectively navigate in this way, the invisible threads we weave support one another to be that love in all of its fullness. And what happens when we've predominantly gone about our lives doing for others and not listening to those unsettled feelings?

I'm not sure.

along the way

Along the way, so very many lose their voice.
Later along the way, some few reclaim it.

While, all the while,
even fewer retain that facet
of physical energy
that brings form to the nonphysical sacred contract.

The agreement of soul with the universe.

The very essence behind each individual incarnation.

It is the energy of the "no two identical snowflakes,"
the energy of the "no two identical any things."

It is of that which we are meant to be.

Our truth.

Singular, yet infinite, sacred and sublime.

It is our voice, the authentic voice of soul.

Along the way, so very many lose their voice. That's what happens. Most of us lose our voice because we are afraid we will hurt someone else's feelings.

I've done that so many times. Now I know that I didn't have the courage to speak what I was truly feeling. I didn't want to stir things up. I remember feeling badly inside, but I wouldn't say something to the other person.

Isn't that interesting? We say we love ourselves, yet we worry more about someone else's feelings than about embracing our own. That's what happens when we are thinking our way rather than feeling our way.

Yes. Feeling not thinking. Now when I am getting that unsettled feeling I reflect on that phrase. It helps me speak my voice and have the courage to take care of myself in the situation.

Later along the way, some few reclaim it. You've come to a point where the unsettled feeling has gotten so loud that you must listen. That feeling is actually the voice of your soul calling out from within. And it's happening for so many. More than ever before we are not only listening to that voice, we are responding. What we are seeing through our individual and collective experiences – our external worlds – are precise reflections of our individual and collective internal struggles. And the situations we see in our daily lives are reflections of that. The invitation is to see that we actually manifest these occurrences as opportunities to heal the **splintered piece of peace [Session Two]**, to reclaim our voices.

While, all the while, even fewer retain that facet of physical energy that brings form to the nonphysical sacred contract. The agreement of soul with the universe. The very essence behind each individual incarnation. Since the dawn of time there have been those enlightened beings who come into this world already expressing the fullness of love. Although these individuals represent each of the different spiritual traditions, their messages are always the same: to be love. They serve as reminders for each of us to see that which we already are; for us to know we are each vessels embodying uniquely sacred pieces of peace.

When science goes out into the virgin snowfield, it confirms **the energy of the "no two identical snowflakes," the energy of the "no two identical any things."** It confirms that in the essentially infinite number of snowflakes there are no two with the identical crystalline pattern. And so as we go out into the virgin snowfields of our lives, the invitation is to see the relationship between the **no two identical snowflakes** and the **no two identical any things;** to see that there are no two identical souls.

The invitation is for each of us to be our fullest expression of soul – to be that singularly unique snowflake in all of its fullness and all of its majesty. **It is of that which we are meant to be. Our truth. Singular, yet infinite, sacred and sublime. It is our voice, the authentic voice of soul.** To be *me, finally.*

> *I was sharing with a friend about my experience with Seeing With Heart and she said, "Your energy is different. It's strong. It's light. It's radiant."*

That's the "flowing over" Seeing With Heart spoke to earlier.

> *(With a deep, gentle sigh.) Yes. I am flowing over. I am so grateful that now I feel less stuffed up and stuck.*

Where did you feel that stuffed up, stuck stuff?

> *(Pointing.) Here, in my throat and upper chest.*

at the very bottom of my throat

At the very bottom of my throat. That's where.

Oh, you feel it now too. Good, that's the first step.

Go ahead, give yourself permission to embrace this place.

I know, it's bitter, really bitter. And sour, even rancid. Bubbling,
yet not moving. It's so stuck.

Finally, you feel the pain. For so long it wasn't allowed to be any part
of you. Huge denial. That's where all of this stuffed stuff hides,
at the very bottom of our throats wrapped so neatly
in the protective satin lining (of denial).

Go ahead, let it go; groan – let it move.
Yes, it burns (on its way out) – it must.

Let the tears flow; the weeping will dilute the burning,
the caustic burning.

Have trust; in time this burning will pass,
for it is only a surface pain.

The deep pain is the "no pain" of the stuffed stuff.
It is the pain that silently kills us all as we live.

Let us seize the opportunity in this moment of awareness.

Let us let go from that very deep place.

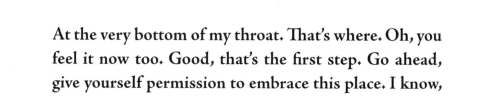

**At the very bottom of my throat. That's where. Oh, you
feel it now too. Good, that's the first step. Go ahead,
give yourself permission to embrace this place. I know,**

it's bitter, really biter. And sour, even rancid. Bubbling, yet not moving. It's so stuck. Doesn't this sound familiar?

Yes. That's what we were just talking about. The stuffed up, stuck stuff.

Finally, you feel the pain. For so long it wasn't allowed to be any part of you. Huge denial. That's where all of this stuffed stuff hides, at the very bottom of our throats wrapped so neatly in the protective satin lining (of denial).

That's right. For so long I didn't even know I was in pain. Then when I began to notice it, I didn't even really know what it was about. Now I'm seeing that this pain is what happens when I'm not caring for myself. It's what happens when I'm always doing for others and not wanting to stir things up or hurt someone else's feelings.

And who are you hurting?

Me!

And what does this pain feel like?

Really bitter. Sometimes it actually feels like a lump of food stuck at the bottom of my throat.

And so the invitation is for each of us to open the aperture, to awaken the love of self, and live beyond fear. **Go ahead, let it go; groan – let it move. Yes, it burns (on its way out) – it must. Let the tears flow; the weeping will dilute the burning, the caustic burning. Have trust; in time this burning will pass, for it is only a surface pain.** Do you know what the tears are?

I'm not sure. Love?

Yes, love. As each one of us opens our aperture, the love that has been welling up begins to move. Initially it burns. And that burning is actually the physical expression of having not honored ourselves, of having not cared for ourselves. Then as we awaken the love of self, the love that has been welling up flows as tears. These tears dilute the caustic burning and the pain lessens. Have you ever noticed how much more comfortable your chest and belly feel after you've had a good cry?

Yes.

That's because the tears are love, and love is healing.

It's remarkable that for so long I didn't even know something was actually troubling me; I didn't feel this burning pain.

The deep pain is the "no pain" of the stuffed stuff. It is the pain that silently kills us all as we live. That's what happens, as the stuffed stuff is literally the invisible cause of our dis-ease. And because we have been seeing through the lens of our ordinary eyes, we are not even aware that dis-ease is occurring. However, the invitation is to blink, shift our perception, and see with other than our ordinary eyes that the dis-ease is actually the physical outcome of the stuffed stuff. And the extent to which we aren't caring for ourselves is the extent to which we precisely manifest emotional and physical disease.

Let us seize the opportunity in this moment of awareness. Let us let go from that very deep place. For when we take even one small step into this awareness, the invisible – the stuffed stuff – shifts to visible, and we flow deeper and deeper from within the potent medicine of caring for self – the potent medicine of "I love me."

For the first time I am having this awareness. For the first time I feel really comfortable saying "I love me."

Another simple phrase to place in our heart pockets is "hug my heart." Like the others, the invitation is to pull out this phrase as a prayerful reminder to "I love me." It's a potent possibility.

each morning

Each morning,

upon rising,

I stretch my arms into the place of truly awakening.

I hug my heart.

Intimate Connection

Hug my heart. Those words are so beautiful. When I heard you say that, I had the feeling of hugging myself from within. It felt comforting.

It's amazing how I am already honoring myself in an entirely new way. I not only know that I have to put my oxygen mask on first, I actually feel comfortable about that. I now find that I'm not as worried about what others say or the judgments I hear. I know that the only thing I can do is be love.

This new way of being you speak about is actually our natural way of being – it is about knowing that we have this possibility always. And at the same time we can't be with everyone in this way. We have the ability to discern rather than find ourselves in those unwanted places of being judged for what we could have done or should have done.

I have often struggled with why we judge each other.

but why do you judge me

But why do you judge me?
Does your heart not feel my compassion?

What blinds your soul from seeing my kindness?
OUCH! Your words, they bite so hard, invisibly bruising.
Why do you hit me in this way?

I know why. You're stuck – stuck big in the fear!

Go ahead or not, it's up to you, go behind this fear,
place your attention on how things are really going in your own life
rather than preoccupying your attention with how you imagine
things are going in mine.

It's not up to me to feel the harmony in your heart, it's up to you.

So free yourself, let go of the fear
and see the sea of peace that lives within your soul,
breathing loving intention into this possibility.

Go ahead, or not!

But why do you judge me? Does your heart not feel my compassion? What blinds your soul from seeing my kindness? So often we're simply trying to be helpful and our actions are misunderstood. And then, **OUCH! Your words, they bite so hard, invisibly bruising. Why do you hit me in this way?**

This feels really familiar and it's really painful. Why do we do this?

I know why. You're stuck – stuck big in the fear! Stuck in the fear of not being good enough, of not being anything enough. And then we end up thinking ourselves crazy – making mountains out of molehills. Our apertures close down and blind us from seeing the kindness. Instead, we judge.

Go ahead or not, it's up to you, go behind this fear, place your attention on how things are really going in your own life rather than preoccupying your attention with how you imagine things are going in mine. Isn't it interesting how we end up distracting ourselves with all the stuff that others are doing rather than looking at our own stuff?

Seeing With Heart invites us to blink once again and ask ourselves a not-so-readily-apparent question: Are the words in this writing speaking to another person or are they speaking to self?

Wow. I hadn't even considered that.

The invitation is to know it is the judgment of self that ends up being projected onto others. For example, when someone says, "I hate you," what they are actually saying is, "I hate me"! Through the illusion of separation, it's more obvious to see this occurring to another person. For example, the uncomfortable situations with your dad were the result of Dad projecting his judgment of self towards you.

Do you mean that all of those unhealthy experiences with Dad weren't about me?

Yes and no. There are two ways to look at each situation. From one perspective those situations are precise reflections of the diameter of Dad's aperture, his acceptance of self, and his unconditional love of self. Remember the diameter of the opening in the Hoover Dam that we spoke about earlier?

Yes.

What did that example help us see?

Even though there is essentially an infinite amount of water – an infinite amount of love – behind the wall, the important thing is what's happening at the aperture.

Yes. When we only access a trickle of our unconditional love from within, we project our conditional love of self onto **someone, somebody, any body, [Session Three]** vulnerable. It's so backwards; because, of course, Dad loves you.

Of course he does. It's so crazy what we do!

Now here's what's even crazier! Looking at the situation from the other side, we see that less-than-preferable occurrences are actually precise reflections of our judgments of self – our *conditional* love of self. They present as opportunities for each of us to heal our **splintered piece of peace [Session Two].**

It's not up to me to feel the harmony in your heart, it's up to you. So free yourself, let go of the fear and see the sea of peace that lives within your soul, breathing loving intention into this possibility. The invitation is for each of us to open our aperture, awaken the love of self, and live beyond fear. **Go ahead, or not!**

> *"Or not" is no longer an option. I see now how my pinched-down aperture affects how much I judge others and, more important, how much I judge myself.*

Yes. And the invitation is to ultimately know that it's the judgment of self that fluctuates the aperture.

Seeing With Heart invites us to consider another simple phrase: "I be love. I be me. I be we." To the extent that *I be love* – to the extent that I flow unconditional love, love without judgment – then *I be me*. And to the extent that *I be me* – to the extent that I awaken the love of self, the love of not judging self – then and only then will *I be we*.

I feel like I'm understanding "I be love" and "I be me." However, I'm not clear about "I be we."

"I be we" is about being in relationship with one another in a new way, a way that honors self and the other person without expectation, without judgment. When we be in this way, we be *me, finally*, and in so doing – we, finally. The question is who in your life offers the greatest opportunity for this new way of relating – the greatest opportunity to shift?

My parents?

Yes! Although every interaction with another person potentially holds the same opportunity, it's in the connections with the ones we love the most that we find the greatest medicine for shift.

I know that it's my parents who trigger my most deep-rooted pain. Throughout my life I've found it really difficult to "be love" when my dad was yelling and my mom was criticizing me. Now I see that they were actually projecting their judgments of themselves onto me. And as Seeing With Heart has helped me to see, when they were tall and I was small I didn't have the ability to take care of myself in those uncomfortable situations. Instead I ended up feeling badly and my aperture pinched down.

Yes. The parent, the life partner, the sibling, the best friend – are illuminating beacons to identify where we are, not where we say we are with our **splintered piece of peace [Session Two]**. These illuminating beacons present as opportunities to honor yourself and them without expectation, without judgment.

> *That's remarkable. I guess it's no coincidence that I'm going to have an opportunity to put this into practice. In a few weeks I'll be living at my parents' house for the first time since high school, and it's causing me a lot of stress. The past two years have been very difficult, and I've been praying to have a healthy, loving relationship with them.*

As we've previously explored, through the illusion of coincidence we experience precisely what we authentically need to heal. In this case, isn't it interesting that shortly after we complete the Seeing With Heart journey, you are going to be with that unsettled piece of peace?

> *Now I see that to build a new way with my parents is not to hope that they will change; it is to be love, to be without expectation and judgment, to embrace the possibility of I be love. I be me. I be we.*

intimate relationships

It's in our intimate relationships,
those spirit connections
whose threads stretch deeply
from within the sacred,
that we find the possibility
for our greatest healing.

Our choice is to embrace that place,
or not.

We all have stories, and it's our natural tendency to place great importance on our stories, especially those stories that involve persons with whom we are closest. That's where we experience the greatest charge. And Seeing With Heart invites us to see that our lives are really not about our stories. I feel to share something. It's a letter:

August 19, 2004

My Dear Brother Eric,

This morning I awoke, because I was woken up, by the sensation of tears gently streaming down my face. And then I heard the sounds of whimpering and realized they were coming from within my being. It was so beautiful to be woken in this way… to feel you so close.

It is the day after I learned of what had occurred while you were climbing at Castle Rock, and it is still early in this shifting energy to fully embrace that we will no longer be able to talk and laugh and cry together in the same way as we had often done. And although it is still early, in my heart, I feel peace. For I know, from the deepest place of my being, the deepest place of compassion – that which needs to be, is, always. And even when it may not taste as I would prefer.

In my heart I feel the possibility exists, for the so very many of those whose lives you have touched, to see that what you were and what you are and what you will continue to be forever, is a beacon. A beacon of what it means to be authentic to your spirit, to be the courage to walk your truth. What it means to truly be your passion. Deciding to move to the mountains of Colorado has always been your dream. Eric, I admire you so deeply... for you manifested your dream. Everyone dreams, and yet so few grow them into being. You did.

And you had the courage to embrace what it means to live your life fully, in the truest sense. Even if that meant living your entire life in but one day, or in but one hour of climbing at the end of one day, or in but one moment of that hour, when you reached even deeper

from within that place of fullness to touch that place
you knew so well while being at one with your climb.
And even if that meant having the courage to embrace
the unfolding mystery in a way that some would see as
"risking" it all.

Eric, you are such a gift. And although I will miss you
deeply and have always felt close with you, I feel you
even closer, now.

I love you.

Your dear brother,
Mitch

(Pausing, we look at each other without speaking for some
time.)

I'm speechless. Would you share what happened?

On August 18, 2004, while seeing patients, I received
a call that my brother was missing. I gathered enough
information to determine that it was likely, and called my
mom. "Mom, it's Mitch. Write this down. Eric is missing."
"What?" she exclaimed. "Write this down." And I shared
the information I had gathered.

While on the phone with Mom, my staff notified me that the person who had first called me about Eric was on the other line. I asked Mom to hold, switched calls, and found out my brother was dead. After consoling that person I asked them to stay on the line, returned to Mom, and had the truly remarkable experience of sharing with her that Eric, her son and my brother, had died.

It was always Eric's dream to move from where our family lives in New England to Colorado. He was quite an accomplished mountain climber, had climbed all over the world, and it was the mountains outside Boulder that moved him the most. After years of holding on to that dream, a fabulous job opportunity presented itself. He came to clarity that he was going to follow his heart. It took a lot of courage.

The plan was for Eric to be in Colorado from Monday through Friday and then we would have a going away party for him on Saturday. After training at his new job on Tuesday, he went to his favorite climbing place, Castle Rock. Instead of technical climbing, Eric walked up the back route to watch the sunset and reflect on his new life and on what happens when you have the courage to follow your dream. Then of all things, he slipped and fell from the summit.

I organized to have Eric's body cremated, and a dear friend of mine who lives in Colorado was able to bring his cremains back East. As planned, we did end up having Eric's going away party on Saturday.

When I had gotten off the phone with my mom, I shared with my office staff what had occurred. At that time I realized I had two options. I could cancel patients and walk out the door or use the situation as an opportunity to be fully present with the experience even though it didn't taste as I would have preferred; to not judge the situation and at the same time be with my feelings; to be love.

I looked out into the waiting room. I saw that the next patient was a person I felt to be with, a gentle soul who I knew would be medicine at that moment. So I invited that person to come in.

What happened next was remarkable. Although moments before I had received what would certainly be considered tragic news, I felt completely calm. I actually felt abundant inner peace. I didn't even feel the need to say, "Oh, guess what I just found out." I simply savored the experience of being present with this gentle, compassionate person. Certainly there was nothing I could do to change the situation, nor was there anything I had to do immediately regarding arrangements for Eric. In that moment what

I did do was remember the words from Seeing With Heart: **It's in our intimate relationships, those spirit connections whose threads stretch deeply from within the sacred, that we find the possibility for our greatest healing. Our choice is to embrace that place, or not.**

SESSION EIGHT

Be Present

(With tears flowing.) I don't even know what to say. I am so moved. Hearing how you embraced that incredibly personal moment in your life really helps me see how to embrace being with my parents in a new way.

Seeing With Heart invites each one of us to have the capacity to be present with what is, even and especially when it does not taste as we would prefer. So the invitation is to be that way with Eric and to be that way with your parents and to be that way with all that we experience.

the bitter screaming gale

From within the bitter screaming gale
the soft tranquil smile tenderly embraces
the cold biting wind
while the warm peaceful heart
gently wraps its loving arms
around all who taste the sweetness
in this bitter screaming gale.

From within the bitter screaming gale is a call for us to embrace the medicine in the excruciating.

Wow. I hadn't even considered that.

It's really easy for us to be peaceful as we take a leisurely stroll along the water's edge at sunset on a warm summer evening. However, the invitation is to be in this way in all of our experiences, no matter the flavor. And **the soft tranquil smile** is actually the physical expression of acceptance. It is the me and the you who **tenderly embraces the cold biting wind.** Remember the tug on the shirt-sleeve?

Yes.

That's **the cold biting wind.** Eric was a fascinating tug. So was your dad. We all experience the fascinating experience of **the cold biting wind.** The question is what do we do with it? Often our initial response is to kick and scream. However, the opportunity is to embody the infinity of love that resides ever-so-slightly behind our beating hearts; to embody the infinity of potential that resides ever-so-slightly behind the walls of our "Hoover Dams." We don't have to find it. It's already there. The opportunity is to be **the warm peaceful heart,** always.

As I look back on my life, I'm now realizing how much I've struggled to be in acceptance – how much I've struggled to be the warm, peaceful heart.

When we struggle to be in acceptance we are unable to be **the soft tranquil smile** and invariably end up tumbling around in **the bitter screaming gale.** Doesn't that feel familiar?

> *Yes. And when those excruciating moments occur, it feels awful. I get so frustrated and wonder how I let it happen again. Now I'm seeing that it really doesn't have to. All I need to do is remind myself to be the soft, tranquil smile — to remind myself to be love.*

Yes. When we embody the infinity of love that resides ever-so-slightly behind our beating hearts, when we be *me, finally,* **the warm peaceful heart gently wraps its loving arms around all who taste the sweetness in this bitter screaming gale.**

> *I'd like to share something that occurred.*

Please.

> *As you were reading Eric's letter and it was becoming clear what had happened, instead of hearing your story I created my own story. I actually started imagining what it would be like if my sister died. Why am I still finding it so hard to stop my mind from creating what is not there?*

Your question illustrates how easy it is to slip back into thinking and not feeling. That's how we end up making mountains out of molehills, making your sister dead, thinking ourselves crazy! When these unsettled situations occur we need to remind ourselves to circle back and revisit earlier Seeing With Heart writings. Remember, **embrace the possibility of not thinking about anything, expanding instead, from within the place of feeling about everything [Session Three].**

> *Thinking myself crazy is exactly what I did. Even though I feel like so much has shifted since beginning the Seeing With Heart journey, I'm amazed at how quickly I went back to thinking and judging myself.*

Seeing With Heart reminds us that we're still early in our experience of embodying the framework, so invariably we'll slip back into the thinking and judging, acknowledging that at times it will feel wobbly. Remember these three simple words: from within without – **from within the place of without expectation [Session One],** especially from within the place of not judging self.

> *Wow. I forgot about "from within without."*

In fact, having the awareness of not judging ourselves when moments before we had judged ourselves is extremely potent medicine. Like athletes, we require training to develop our spiritual skills. Embodying the framework that we spoke of earlier is about making commitments to ourselves to do spiritual "push-ups." And because of how accessible and effective Seeing With Heart is, within a very short period of time the number of push-ups increases exponentially.

> *That's so interesting. I hadn't even thought about training to develop my spiritual skills.*

The possibility is to live our training in each and every moment as waking, walking, and breathing meditations. Training is the action of reaching into our heart pockets for support in real time and using *blink, feeling not thinking, from within without, reclaiming voice, I love me, the fluctuating aperture,* and all of the building blocks as we navigate life.

As part of our training, Seeing With Heart invites us to keep track of how many times we say something self-defeating or complain about the weather, the news, a co-worker, or a family member. Invite yourself to check in regularly and observe how rapidly shift occurs. Know that as we change our language, we change that which we resonate. With each breath we take, the possibility is to resonate in this new way.

let us relish the cycle

Let us relish the cycle,
the cycle of the breathing,
the conduit that is both
the weaver and the weaving.

So effortlessly drawing intention
into each facet of this glittering jewel,
the breathing reminds us that
as we wander along the path,
our work
is to play.

For as we move within its current
we are called to rest often in its eddies,
to imperceptibly inhale the intoxicating illuminations,
caress the undulating tendrils of the iridescent moon rays
and savor, ever so slowly, the succulent dewdrops of dawn.

And so, let us relish both
the weaver and the weaving,
in this eternal rhythmic cycle
of the breathing.

Hmmm. Our work is to play. It reminds me of when we were young and on Saturday mornings we couldn't wait to get up and clean the house because we made it a game. We walked around with our wooden spoons and pans singing

songs as we cleaned. It was so much fun and at the same time it was work.

The breathing reminds us that as we wander along the path, our work is to play. As we wander through life, the possibility is to embrace each breath as that sacred reminder to find joy in all. And to have the awareness that with each breath we are **both the weaver** – the infinity of potential, **and the weaving** – the expression of that potential.

So are you saying that each one of us is a weaver, and depending on what we do with our aperture, we directly affect our weaving?

Yes. And as we step deeper and deeper from within this new way of embracing the **eternal rhythmic cycle of the breathing,** the texture of the weaving – the texture of life – becomes an ever-more-radiant expression of our collective awakening.

Wow. I can really see how simply bringing awareness to my breath is a potent reminder to be present.

so what did i do

So what did I do through this time called today?

Embrace in the sacred and sip in the moment,
while playing with shadows as they dance with the earth?

Touch the deep mystery by watching a squirrel, a finch, and
a heron, an egret, a rose? A tulip, an orchid, so yellow and crimson
and lavender and scarlet and orange and blue,
and fortunately I forgot not to take in the dew.

The moonrise, the sunset, the song of the breeze,
the sweet wash of nectar so anxious to please.

But oh, now I ponder as my day draws to close,
did I tenderly touch all these morsels of magic?
Or did I just push through my day as a struggle,
a battle to win, just a foe for the conquer –
rushing and blinding the splendor of moment
and stumbling along with my eyes so wide shut?

So what did I do through this time called *today*? The
invitation is to be present, to be the same expression
of love whether you're washing the dishes or sharing a
special moment with someone you love. The possibility
is to **embrace in the sacred and sip in the moment,** no
matter the flavor. However, the question to ask ourselves
is **did I just push through my day as a struggle, a battle
to win, just a foe for the conquer – rushing and blinding**

the splendor of moment and stumbling along with my
eyes so wide shut?

*Prior to Seeing With Heart I did struggle, and missed so
much. Now I find myself being more present and more
accepting of unsettling situations. But what if it hurts?
What about my feelings?*

Those are great questions. We need to feel our feelings.
Otherwise **the stuffed stuff** – our feelings – **hides at the
very bottom of our throats wrapped so neatly in the
protective satin lining (of denial) [Session Six].**

**For the deep pain is the "no pain" of the stuffed stuff. It
is the pain that silently kills us all as we live [Session
Six].** It's actually essential for our spiritual, emotional,
and physical well-being to give ourselves permission to
embrace the whimpering, the tears, the painful places.
And when we do, we cultivate inner peace.

peace and light
May peace and light be your chariot,
as that which needs to be, is,
always.

129

Yes... that which needs to be, is, always. (Whispers contemplatively while nodding her head.)

SESSION NINE
Situation Spiral

Good morning!

I sense an excitement that you have something to share.

Yes! Last night, before bedtime, I journaled and I feel to read what I wrote.

I would love that.

"It's time to blink and be me, finally. It's time to listen to the unsettled feelings I've felt for so long. Throughout my life I've often felt an ache in my heart and didn't listen. I've tried so many times to shift and couldn't. I figured it was the way my life was meant to be.

Seeing With Heart has already helped me see a new way of being, a new way of loving myself. Now, as unsettled situations occur, I actually blink and see a new way of looking at things. I like knowing that I have a heart pocket filled with simple building blocks. They're really helpful! It's amazing how quickly my life is shifting!"

That's huge.

It is huge! It's amazing how I'm already feeling so much less overwhelmed. When unsettled situations arise, I've been able to move through them with much greater ease.

Now let's explore the relationship between the unsettled feelings that have been so prevalent throughout your life and the unsettled situations that continue to occur.

situations and dramas

Situations and dramas,
those moments in life
that are often considered problem and conflict
(at times even catastrophe)
are actually the voice of our nonphysical energy
calling out through the illusion
of physical experience.

These moments show up proportionate to
and frequently larger than
the piece of splintered soul.

Unsettled feelings are the visceral sensations in the pits of our stomachs that we often neglect. And when we do, we invariably end up in those **unwanted places – those** situations we prefer to not really be in [Session Six]. These feelings are our inner voices calling for us to listen. **From afar, a child calls, from behind the breeze and before the waves. Listen, for it is truth [Session Two].** They are the actual internal physical experiences of the aperture. When it's narrow, we feel the aches in our hearts. When it's open, we feel the much greater ease.

Unsettled situations are what happen when we neglect the unsettled feelings and don't listen to our inner voices. That's when we inevitably manifest the **situations and dramas, those moments in life that are often considered problem and conflict (at times even catastrophe).** So each unsettled situation, each problem, each catastrophe is an actual external physical experience of the aperture as it fluctuates.

That which we see is a precise reflection of that which we be. So as we expand the bandwidth and see with the entire eighty-eight notes of the piano rather than the eight notes in the middle, we see that the unsettled feelings **are actually the voice of our nonphysical energy calling out through the illusion of physical experience,** manifesting as unsettled situations. **These moments show up proportionate to and frequently larger than the piece of splintered soul.** To this point the predominant paradigm has been for us to experience these moments with charge.

That's the "banging our heads against the wall" that each of us knows so well. The invitation, however, is to see that we manifest these unsettled situations as the gentle and sometimes not-so-gentle tugs on our shirt-sleeves.

I didn't get in a car accident. Eric didn't accidentally slip and fall. There are no accidents. This brings us back to earlier in our journey when Seeing With Heart invited us to see the patterns in what appears to be patternless. Even though occurrences appear to be unrelated, there are no random, discrete events – no coincidences. Unsettled situations are the illuminating beacons in the fogs of our lives that let us see where we are, not where we say we are.

The possibility is to see that **situations and dramas, those moments in life that are often considered problem and conflict (at times even catastrophe),** are the blessed blessings, the potent medicine.

> *These words are profound. I never really considered embracing unsettled situations as medicine. In the past they were always problems. Now I am seeing the relationship between how I fluctuate my aperture and what is actually occurring in my life. I'm seeing that when I listen to the feeling in the pit of my stomach and love myself without judgment, I don't end up in the unwanted places. It's blink!*

Yes. It is blink. As we considered earlier in our journey, how we gaze at the "artwork" of our lives – the gray areas, the way that we squint and tip our heads to one side or the other – determines our perception. At times we see fish swimming, and when we blink, without going anywhere, we see birds flying. Seeing With Heart is not asking us to move up or down in our lives; it simply invites us to blink and see that there is another option – the possibility to see the medicine in the excruciating.

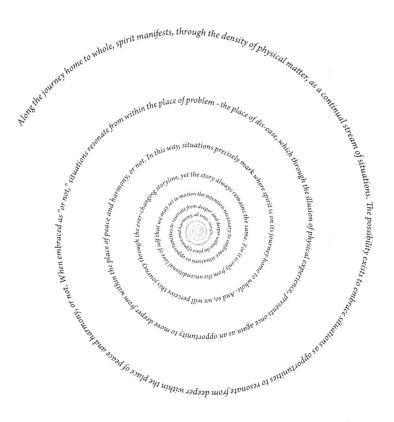

Look at how this writing showed up.

It's a spiral!

Yes. With only two exceptions, all of the writings revealed themselves in vertical columns. With this one I found myself rotating the page as words appeared.

That's fascinating!

It is. This is the "Situation Spiral." As we embody the message in its words and the swirling pattern of their orientation, we see how Seeing With Heart illuminates a not-so-readily-apparent pattern about how each of our lives unfolds.

situation spiral

Along the journey home to whole, spirit manifests, through the density of physical matter, as a continual stream of situations. The possibility exists to embrace situations as opportunities to resonate from deeper within the place of peace and harmony, or not. When embraced as "or not," situations resonate from within the place of problem – the place of dis-ease, which through the illusion of physical experience, presents once again as an opportunity to move deeper from within the place of peace and harmony, or not. In this way, situations precisely mark where spirit is on its journey home to whole. And so, we will perceive this journey through the ever-changing storyline, yet the story always remains the same. For it is only from the unconditional love of self that we may set in motion the intention necessary to embrace situations as opportunities to resonate from deeper and deeper within the place of peace and harmony, all ways.

Along the journey home to whole is the call from spirit to be **the authentic voice of soul [Session Six].** As we individually and collectively awaken to this awareness – to our natural ways of being, we each come to a place in our life where this inner calling is so strong that we simply have no other option than to listen. We find the courage and the love of self to be that which we are meant to be.

> *Prior to this journey, I had been feeling a calling and did not know what to do. Now I see that it was the unsettled feelings nagging at my very core. They were screaming at me and I couldn't ignore them anymore. It's literally why I'm making the Seeing With Heart journey.*

And as we go **along the journey home to whole,** the invitation is to see that spirit is the invisible essence, the nonphysical energy behind all that we see; that through all of the "every things" and all of the random, unrelated occurrences in our lives, **spirit manifests, through the density of physical matter,** through the lens of our ordinary eyes, the eight notes, **as a continual stream of situations.**

When we blink and see through the lens of other than our ordinary eyes, the lens of all eighty-eight notes, we see that **the possibility exists to embrace situations,** no matter the flavor, **as opportunities to resonate from deeper within the place of peace and harmony;** to embrace all of the every things and all of the unrelated occurrences as opportunities to be present. **Or not.**

When embraced as "or not," situations resonate from within the place of problem – the place of dis-ease, which through the illusion of physical experience, presents once again as an opportunity to move deeper from within the place of peace and harmony, or not. When embraced as "or not" – the place of problem – we immediately experience the swirling, the "repeatedly banging our heads against the walls" dis-ease that we all know so well.

Have you ever reflected on how you felt when you found yourself in one of those **unwanted places [Session Six]**?

Yes.

And what does it feel like?

Dizzying. At times my head feels like it's spinning. It actually hurts!

Exactly. **The place of dis-ease** is what happens when we're in our heads thinking ourselves crazy, making mountains out of molehills. The invitation is to see that each of our lives is a Situation Spiral. In one moment we embrace situations as opportunities and feel expanding ease, while in the next moment we embrace them as problems and feel dis-ease. We're spinning our lives around and around and around the spiral. It's like that ride in the playground with a flat, circular surface for standing and some bars for bracing. When we're safely sitting near the center, it doesn't matter how fast the ride spins. However, when we're out towards the edge, we literally get thrown off. This is what we do in our lives. We live the Situation Spiral.

In this way, situations precisely mark where spirit is on its journey home to whole. They mark where we are, not where we say we are. **Situations precisely mark** how we are individually and collectively fluctuating the aperture.

And so, we will perceive this journey through the ever-changing storyline, yet the story always remains the same. The storylines – the ever-changing events in our lives – are precise physical reflections of the story – the love of self. And depending on how we individually and collectively fluctuate the aperture, we literally manifest, through the ever-changing storyline, different versions of the same story.

Instead of getting ourselves caught up in the storyline – "Did I get hired?" "Did I get fired?" – know that it's what we do with the story – our love of self – that affects the storyline. The invitation is to see that the storyline is never about the storyline; it's about the story. The invitation is to see that we create the infinity of ever-changing storylines to heal our stories – to heal the love of self. In fact, we all have different storylines and yet we all have the same story. **For it is only from the unconditional love of self that we may set in motion the intention necessary to embrace situations as opportunities to resonate from deeper and deeper within the place of peace and harmony, all ways.**

It's like the original *Mission Impossible* television series and each one of us is Mr. Phelps receiving our instructions before "the tape self-destructs in five seconds." Each and every situation, each and every random storyline, is actually our assignment to accept, or not. Why else would we be having these experiences we call life? To get the stuff? To get the things? No! It is to BE LOVE; to be the fullest expression of the infinite potential that lies within each of us.

SESSION TEN

Situation Sphere

As I was journaling last night, I found myself whispering,
"I be love."

How did that feel?

It felt like I was hugging my heart, like I was loving me.
Then I found myself writing about my feelings. This is
an enormous shift, as in the past I would write about my
situations and dramas – the storyline. Now I am seeing
that the storyline is a reflection of my story – my love of self;
and since my love of self has changed, so has my storyline.

It's so important to embody this subtle yet significant awareness. **The storyline is always changing yet the story always remains the same [Session Nine].** No matter what we are doing, our storylines can always be related back to the same story – the love of self.

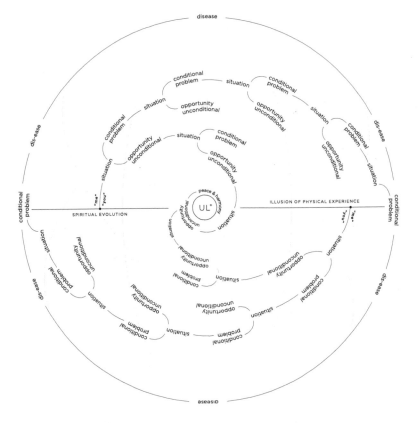

*UL = unconditional love

Wow. What's this?

The "Situation Sphere." This is the other exception in the writings, and it represents an expanding, three-dimensional, spherical shape.

It looks confusing.

Initially it might seem to be. Soon you'll see that it's simple to understand, and at the same time its message is profound. What do you see written below the horizontal line that runs across this image?

"Spiritual evolution."

And when you continue along the line, what else do you see written?

"Illusion of physical experience."

How can one line have two labels? How can the same line represent two different concepts?

Seeing With Heart invites us to see that they are actually not two different concepts. Instead they are two ways of referring to the same concept: that which we see is a precise reflection of that which we be. So through the illusion of physical experience, through all of our **situations and dramas [Session Nine],** we are actually witnessing spiritual evolution; we are seeing a precise reflection of spirit **along the journey home to whole [Session Nine].**

That's really fascinating. And what about the dots?

The dots illustrate two hypothetical scenarios. One dot is located in the middle of the line as it goes out from the center to the left. That dot is labeled "me" and "you."

We also observe on the line going out from the center to the right, near the outer perimeter, that there is another dot with the same labels: "me" and "you." Also notice that along the perimeter line we see the words "conditional," "dis-ease," and "disease." And in the very center, "UL" represents unconditional love. Does anything come into your awareness as you reflect on this image?

> *The farther we are from the center – unconditional love – the more we are out at the perimeter – conditional love. So the more conditional love, the more dis-ease. It's like the playground ride.*

Exactly. And the dots – the "me" and "you" – are just two of the infinite number of dots along the horizontal line – the infinite number of ways that the "we" interacts through the illusion of physical experience along our spiritual evolution.

The "me"-and-"you" dot to the left is centered between the perimeter and "UL" to illustrate an equal amount of conditional and unconditional love being expressed, while the "me"-and-"you" dot to the right is closer to the outer perimeter, representing a significantly greater amount of conditional love being expressed. These hypothetical examples illustrate two discernibly different life situations. Can you guess which one is more uncomfortable?

Yes, the one to the right.

Why?

Because the more we live in judgment and expectation, the greater the conditional love and dis-ease.

And where we are on the line – the precise ratio of conditional and unconditional love as it flows out through the you and the me – precisely determines our interactions, our actual life experiences **through the ever-changing storyline [Session Nine].**

The question to ask ourselves is "What ratio are we flowing?" Is it 60 percent unconditional love and 40 percent conditional love? Or is it 40-60? Is it 90-10 or 10-90? 37-63? 50-50? The invitation is to see that all of the seemingly unrelated storylines – all of the random coincidences in our lives – are precise reflections of the precise proportional ratio of the story – the love of self. So here's another question: What do you see when the "me" and the "you" move away from the center horizontal line?

I see the word situation with curved lines branching off in two directions.

Yes. As the "me" and the "you" move away from the line, as we interact with each other and with ourselves, we actually manifest situations. These situations occur as illuminating beacons – tugs on our shirt-sleeves – for us to see where we are, not where we say we are **along the journey home to whole [Session Nine].** The possibility exists to see that as we go along our lives – as we laugh, cry, dance, argue, embrace, and touch in ever-so-many ways – we manifest a **continual stream of situations [Session Nine]** as opportunities – unconditional love – to become the fullest expressions of ourselves. All ways. Or not.

When embraced as "or not," we manifest situations as problems – conditional love. We either move closer to the center of our true place of being – peace and harmony – or we swirl ourselves outward to dis-ease. For example, let's say we plan a day at the beach and it ends up raining. We often embrace those "rainy days" with judgment and find ourselves saying, "It wasn't supposed to rain." "It's such a lousy day." On the other hand, the possibility exists to embrace unsettled situations with acceptance, as opportunities, and enjoy getting the projects done that we've been putting off for that rainy day. Which way of being would you prefer?

Opportunity! It's so clear to me now that in the past I predominantly embraced unsettled situations as problems, whether I spilled a cup of tea on my clothes, was late for an important meeting because I was stuck in traffic, or, like you said, got really upset that it was raining when I had plans for a beach day. Now I'm realizing how much time I've spent spinning myself outward to dis-ease.

Yes. We do this all the time.

I can really see how what we are doing in our lives is like that ride at the playground. I am actually getting the feeling of what the 70-30 ride feels like as compared to the 30-70 ride. The visual image of the Situation Sphere is helping me see how I fluctuate my aperture.

The Situation Sphere is an easy way to see how we individually and collectively create conflict and dis-ease or peace and harmony. It also illustrates the direct connection between our *spirit dis-ease* and the emotional and physical diseases we experience.

I've been wondering why the word disease was on the outer perimeter line. Do you mean this has something to do with why we get sick?

Yes. When we live with a greater percentage of dis-ease – conditional love – we eventually, through the illusion of physical experience, create disease. For example, when we're thinking ourselves crazy, making mountains out of molehills, we often end up with insomnia, migraines, and stomach ulcers.

That's right. I can think of so many restless nights when I tossed and turned because I was thinking myself crazy, and woke up with a headache. I never even considered the relationship between how I judge things and why I get sick. It makes so much sense.

Yes, it really does. As *spirit dis-ease* dissolves, emotional and physical disease resolves.

That's such an intriguing way to look at sickness.

Now Seeing With Heart asks another question: What else might the infinite number of dots – the "me" and "you" along the horizontal line – represent?

You mean something besides "spiritual evolution" and "illusion of physical experience"?

Yes.

I'm not sure.

All right. I'll give you a hint: **Along the journey home to whole, spirit manifests, through the density of physical matter, as a continual stream of situations [Session Nine].**

That's the first line in the Situation Spiral.

Exactly.

So each dot on the horizontal line also represents a Situation Spiral?

Yes. The words **Along the journey home to whole** move away from each dot following the curved lines, and the words **within the place of peace and harmony, all ways** spiral into the very center. How we move along our lives and embrace the situations we manifest precisely determines how we move along the curved lines and to what extent we move closer to or farther away from our true natures – peace and harmony.

That's crazy!

It is.

Following the curved lines is so helpful in seeing how our lives change depending on which paths we embrace.

Here's another question: How many Situation Spirals reside in the Situation Sphere?

A lot?

An infinite number. Well, at least seven billion, as that's the current population of embodied souls on earth, and the number is ever expanding. Isn't it interesting that the Situation Sphere represents an expanding three-dimensional sphere? The invitation is to visualize an essentially infinite number of lines bisecting the sphere in every possible plane of orientation, each comprised of an essentially infinite number of Situation Spirals. Where there is intersection, there is interaction. Where there is interaction, there is co-creation. Where there is co-creation, there is acceptance, expectation, ease, dis-ease, health, disease.

So each of our lives is represented by a Situation Spiral?

Exactly. And no matter where we are on our individual and collective journeys, within each of us resides the infinite potential to manifest expanding peace and harmony, all ways.

Now Seeing With Heart asks us to explore an even more subtle aspect of the Situation Sphere: Why is it an expanding three-dimensional sphere?

I don't know.

Hasn't science "established" that the universe is expanding?

Yes.

And science invites us to consider that almost fourteen billion years ago a very prominent event occurred that relates to this expanding.

The Big Bang.

So what does the Situation Sphere represent?

The Big Bang?

Yes.

What?!

Yes. Seeing With Heart invites us to consider that each one of us is simultaneously manifesting our own singularly unique "Big Bang." Individually we literally create the universe that we see, the universe that we be. Remember, that which we see is a precise reflection of that which we be.

That's mind-boggling! I'm not even sure how to respond.

Let's take a closer look. Since our predominant way of seeing has been from within the narrow bandwidth, we see an essentially infinite number of yesterdays and tomorrows. Hence we look out into space and see evidence of the singular "yesterday" event we have labeled the Big Bang. However, when we invite ourselves to blink, to expand the bandwidth and embody that there is ever so much more occurring than we see through our ordinary eyes, we see that individually and collectively we are actually creating the illusion of that yesterday called "fourteen billion years ago" – the event labeled the Big Bang. So everything we are doing and everything we are seeing are precise reflections of our unique individual and collective Big Bangs. And the event we have labeled the Big Bang is actually a precise reflection of our individual and collective love of self. As we blink and fully embody that we are literally manifesting our individual universes, Seeing With Heart invites us to ponder this question: Who wrote the original Seeing With Heart writings?

(Pondering.) Me?

Yes. You did. Literally. Remember this passage from early in our journey – **These words are not "mine," yet they have the illusion of flowing through me. Instead, they are core truths that resonate from within each of us. If I felt they were mine, the possibility for receiving them would be not [Session One].**

Who wrote this book that you're reading?

I did!

Who created the Seeing With Heart journey?

I did! It's my journey.

That's right.

And it's our journey.

That's right. I be love...

...I be me. I be we. (Speaking simultaneously.)

Stillness

As I was climbing into bed last night, I realized something fascinating.

What?

Well, picture this. I sleep on a floating bed. It's a round platform suspended by lines attached to the perimeter, which are secured at a single point in the ceiling. The bed is free-swinging.

Wow. That sounds like an amazing way to sleep.

It is. And what's really amazing is how my bed reminds me of the Situation Sphere.

Really?

Yes! When you first climb in, it has a rocking motion. Then it spirals around until it finally goes still.

How is that like the Sphere?

I am realizing that when I first "climbed" into this journey,

I felt a lot of rocking, a lot of dis-ease. When I was embracing unsettled situations as problems, I was living out towards the perimeter of the Sphere. Now that I am seeing opportunities in what I had previously considered problems, I am moving toward the center of the Sphere and find my life becoming the same stillness I feel when my bed stops rocking.

dancing in stillness

Dancing in stillness in the nectar of bliss,
the hummingbird motionlessly courts the orchid,
fully embracing the intimacy of interdependence.

Nothing escapes this sharing – this connection – of nourishment and fertility; nectar and seed.

And so the hummingbird and orchid
passionately stir our souls,
ever-so-brightly illuminating the path.

The path calling us to the dancing in stillness in the nectar of bliss.

Wow. These words speak directly to the stillness I am feeling. However, I never thought of dancing in stillness. When I think of dance, I think of movement.

Dancing in stillness in the nectar of bliss calls us to see that as we "dance," as we move about our lives, it's from within the stillness – from within the "no dance" – that we flow peace and harmony, that we flow *love*.

And what about **the hummingbird motionlessly courts the orchid?** Even though its wings beat at up to 200 times per second, its body is often absolutely motionless. The hummingbird elegantly reminds us that no matter how fast-paced, how harried our lives are, the possibility is to be motionless, to be stillness. For it is from within this stillness that the hummingbird and orchid are **fully embracing the intimacy of interdependence.** We see clearly how their relationship is effortless. And how from this way of being, our relationships can be effortless. We see clearly how **nothing escapes this sharing – this connection – of nourishment and fertility; nectar and seed.**

And so the hummingbird and orchid passionately stir our souls, ever-so-brightly illuminating the path. The path calling us to the dancing in stillness in the nectar of bliss.

The invitation for each of us as we move along our paths – our singularly unique Situation Spirals – is to flow from within that stillness; to flow our lives from within the center of the Situation Sphere. That's why it feels so very sweet when your floating bed goes still.

Authentic Power

"In the stillness of the moment hides the infinity of the joy."

You're still pondering these words.

Yes. I'm reflecting on how often along our journey Seeing With Heart has said so much to me with so few words. Now I'm realizing the reason I feel this way is because these words are mine – they really are my core truths.

Yes, **they are core truths that resonate from within each of us [Session One].** How does it feel to know that?

I feel an ease in my chest – an inner strength that I did not know was there. Right now it feels like that deep stillness I feel when my bed stops rocking. I'm feeling love flowing out from my heart.

Are you aware of something that shifted for you to feel this way?

Knowing that everything I experience is flowing out from within me, from within the deep stillness of my infinite well. In fact, it reminds me of the writing "It's not about the outside, or even reaching to the in, for to taste the peace of love, sip the seeing from within."

As we've explored, we never find peace by looking outside of ourselves – by seeing through the narrow bandwidth.

step out from the box

Step out from the box,
as it's steeped so in fear,
and embrace the flow
of expanding from within;
know that there's nowhere
to go to get there,
for you're already home;
when you're happy, you're "you."

The possibility is for each of us to **step out from the box, the narrow bandwidth, as it's steeped so in fear, and embrace the flow of expanding from within** – embrace the flow from within the infinite potential that resides within each of us. And **know that there's nowhere to go to get there, for you're already home; when you're happy, you're "you."** This is a call to know that there is nowhere to go; that **it's not about the outside [Session**

Three]. It's a call for each of us to flow from within our infinite well and be our fullest potential.

The more I realize that the call is about me being me, the more I love who I am. I used to think that was such a horrible thing. Now I feel comfortable saying, "I love who I am!" I've never said that before.

You're not alone. This way of being – of not feeling comfortable acknowledging self – is so common. It's not only okay to "love who I am," it's essential. Remember the writing **Each morning, upon rising, I stretch my arms into the place of truly awakening. I hug my heart [Session Six].** What happens when we stutter-step and lose our "love of who I am" – when we lose our place of stillness?

We lose our power. It leaks out.

empower the drama

Empower the drama
and the power leaks free
from the compassion with boundaries;
the compassion with "me."

Show up instead
with the authentic power
of without expectation;
the true power of "we."

That's amazing. Moments ago I was speaking about how we lose our power, how it leaks out. And then you read those exact words: "the power leaks free"! Before my experience with Seeing With Heart I would have exclaimed, "That's such a coincidence!" Now I am seeing how I directly manifest these coincidences. It reminds me of when you talked about seeing the patterns in what previously appeared patternless.

And how does this relate to your love of self and your aperture?

The more I love myself, the more it opens. And the more it opens, the more often I see the patterns in what I had previously considered coincidences.

Yes. What you are speaking to illustrates what happens as we fluctuate the ratio of unconditional love to conditional love. It illustrates how the love of self directly affects all that we see.

So when we stutter-step and lose our "love of who I am," we **empower the drama and the power leaks free.** Remember, the invitation is to see that all of the seemingly unrelated storylines – all of the random coincidences in our lives – are precise reflections of the precise proportional ratio of the story – the love of self.

> *Yes, I am really seeing that the more I judge myself, the more my aperture pinches down. And the more it pinches down, the more I empower the drama and the power leaks free.*

And what about **the compassion with boundaries; the compassion with "me"**? What are you to do when the oxygen masks deploy?

> *Put my mask on first!*

Interesting. That's exactly the opposite of the answer you gave at the beginning of our journey.

> *Now I know that inner peace is about taking care of myself and loving myself in a way that I hold safe boundaries. I'm finally realizing that I can't be good for anybody else unless I reach for my oxygen mask first.*

And what happens when you do?

I feel empowered.

I'm hearing for us to do an exercise. Let's stand facing each other with our feet shoulder-width apart. With your permission, I'm going to apply a light pressure with my pinky finger to your upper chest. ...What happened?

I wobbled and fell back.

Does that feel like the power you have been feeling?

No.

Okay. Now move your left foot forward and your right one back, making sure that both knees are slightly bent. Now I'll use the back of my hand and do the same thing. ...What happened?

Nothing. And you used a lot more pressure. My body feels strong and stable.

Yes. When we stand flat-footed in life, with stiff knees, we wobble and fall back. And when that occurs, the invitation is to change our stance and stand in our authentic power.

I'm seeing that nothing is going to push me over when I'm standing in this new way of being.

Show up instead with the authentic power of without expectation; the true power of "we." As we approach the culmination of our Seeing With Heart journey, it's interesting to find that these words offer the same message as the first writing we spoke about when we began our journey: **From within the place of without expectation, the universe manifests expanding peace and harmony, always and in all ways [Session One].**

Yes they do. However, I didn't understand them then as I do now.

What do you mean?

Well, I feel like we've been assembling a jigsaw puzzle. And when we only had a few pieces in place, all I saw were the individual messages in those few separate pieces. Now I am seeing how everything is interrelating. I am seeing the whole picture. I am seeing that we truly have assembled a light, accessible, effective framework.

So what does the picture look like?

The Situation Sphere! Except that there are little people instead of dots. And there are scenes of life experiences along the curved lines. Even though I had initially felt that the Situation Sphere was confusing, I am seeing how it incorporates so many essential concepts in such a simple picture. I am seeing that everything I see relates to my love of self.

Like Seeing With Heart invited us to do at the very beginning of our journey, let's close our eyes and open our hearts in a way that to this point we might not have even dreamed possible. I'd like to reread one of the writings.

Okay.

Everything begins with loving the self, yet we're so terribly afraid of "I love me." We listen instead to the voice that's so haunting, the one from so far away. "Don't be so selfish, you must think of the others, and don't hug yourself or spend time with your soul. For remember there's nothing to show from these pleasures, nothing productive, nothing to weigh." "No!" cries your spirit. "This is not about selfish, it's about the importance of caring for self. And doing exactly what one needs in the moment, by feeling with gut, the feeling of true." For being authentic with spirit and soul is the one single choice that will move us to whole. Only then can "I love me" and can "I love you" as they're actually but one in the same [Session Six].

(With tears of joy.) Everything does begin with loving the self, and now I'm not afraid of "I love me." In fact, I love me, finally.

As ripples move outward when dropping a pebble into still water, so do we create ripples when cultivating inner peace, and these ripples manifest an expanding wave of world peace.

—Dr. Mitch Tishler

Points to Ponder

The following points are offered to enhance book group discussions, journaling, and meditation. The invitation is to embrace these points, as they will support you in applying the potent medicine of Seeing With Heart.

Note: To receive a printable copy of the Points to Ponder and the Seeing With Heart eBook – the complete collection of the original channeled writings – please visit www.mefinally.com/readergift.

Session One ~ Embrace the Possibility

Reflect on how *blink* has been paradigm-shifting in your life.

Session Two ~ Paradigmatic Shift

As you begin to see with eighty-eight notes rather than only the eight notes in the middle, how does your perception shift regarding uncomfortable situations?

What have you discovered from the *tugs on your shirt-sleeve?*

Session Three ~ To Journey from Within

As you shift from doing what you think you should do, to doing what you're feeling to do, what do you notice?

Are you predominantly feeling or thinking right now? How do you know?

Reflect on what happens when you look for peace outside of yourself.

Session Four ~ Flow from Within

What happens when you *blink* and see yourself *flowing from within?*

How has the awareness of having a *fluctuating aperture* shifted your life?

Session Five ~ Illusion of Separation

Explore the connection between *the invisible threads, the fluctuating aperture,* and the "coincidences" in your life.

How does *it's never about what it's about* relate to the illusion of separation?

Session Six ~ Love of Self

How does it feel when you say, "I love me"?

What happens in your life when you see that *it's not about selfish, it's about the importance of caring for self?*

Session Seven ~ Intimate Connection

Why is it that your closest relationships provide the greatest opportunity to heal your *splintered piece of peace?*

Explore how "*I be love. I be me. I be we.*" speaks to your relationships with others and, more important, your relationship with yourself.

Session Eight ~ Be Present

What occurs when you embrace the *bitter screaming gale* – the medicine in the excruciating?

Session Nine ~ Situation Spiral

Reflect on how you feel when you *blink* and see that there are no problems.

How does the Situation Spiral support you in seeing that it's never about the storyline, rather it's only ever about the story – the love of self?

Session Ten ~ Situation Sphere

How does the ratio of conditional and unconditional love that you flow affect how you move along the Situation Sphere?

Explore the pattern that emerges as you look at your entire life along the Situation Sphere?

Session Eleven ~ Stillness

Reflect on what occurs when you navigate life with an open heart and access *the infinite well* – the infinity of love that already resides within you.

What do *dancing in stillness* and *the sound of one hand clapping* invite you to embrace?

Session Twelve ~ Authentic Power

Reflect on how the Seeing With Heart journey has supported you in stepping into your authentic power – the power of *Me, Finally*.

Acknowledgments

I didn't grow up dreaming that I would write a book. So as I find myself making final preparations for publication, I pause in humble gratitude for those angels whose input literally breathed life into *Me, Finally*.

At the very top of this list is Debbie Mead. As manager of my wellness center for the past twenty-five years, Debbie has always been my steadfast rudder. After I had been presenting Seeing With Heart for a number of years, Debbie began suggesting I write a book that interpreted the original channeled writings so the potent medicine of Seeing With Heart could be shared with more people.

I would chuckle and say, "That's funny. I thought only authors write books." Two years ago, I heard a voice in my heart. "Listen to Debbie." So with an open heart that's what I did and words flowed out through my fingers. This time I found myself typing on my laptop rather than writing with a pen held in my non-dominant hand, however the experience was virtually the same.

And for the next two years Debbie tirelessly met with me at the office at six a.m. to review the material I had written the night before. We would continue again at lunchtime, and on countless evenings and weekends. Debbie's input was integral to developing a clear voice for *Me, Finally*.

I also express my deepest gratitude to my publisher, Lynne Klippel, who supported me in so many ways along this journey. Most important was the respect Lynne offered to Seeing With Heart's voice, always taking care to retain the essence of the original writings.

It was such a pleasure working with my editor, Gwen Hoffnagle, whose patience and skills were remarkable. *Me, Finally* would not be what it is without her meticulous attention to detail and proficient input.

Special recognition goes to the cover and interior design team, 2Faced Design.com, and David Redondo for their contributions to making *Me, Finally* look so beautiful.

Sincere appreciation to the artist Carmelo Blandino for his blessings to use his exquisite painting, *The Way of Prayer*, on the front cover. Carmelo's artwork expresses the very energetic essence of Seeing With Heart on so many levels.

Warm thanks to my friend Joe Baxter for his artistic input, and to each of my friends (you know who you are) for all your loving support.

To those of you whose hearts and lives have been touched by Seeing With Heart, I am eternally grateful. For it is from your calling to make this journey that the potent medicine of Seeing With Heart continues to more fully emerge.

An extra special expression of gratitude to my dearest friend Michele Insley for always being available no matter the question, no matter the hour. And of course for your amazingly nourishing meals when my refrigerator was empty, which was often, and apparently not uncommon for someone writing a book.

My life is so very blessed by my mom, Sheila; brother, Jason; and former wife, Melissa – and by my brother, Eric, and my Dad, Irving, whose beautiful spirits will forever shine their light from within my heart.

And I close with the deepest expression of love to my daughter, Brielle, and son, Bryce, for all the magical moments we share. I am so blessed to be a part of your lives.

About the Author

Mitch Tishler, D.C., has presented Seeing With Heart™ – a paradigm-shifting program for cultivating inner peace – to individuals and groups internationally since 2000. Mitch holds a Bachelor of Science Degree with an emphasis in genetics from Connecticut College. He earned his Doctor of Chiropractic Degree from National University of Health Sciences in Chicago, Illinois. Before opening his Wellness Center in Chatham, Massachusetts, in 1987, Mitch backpacked with his former wife through North America, New Zealand, Australia, Asia, and Europe for twelve months, often staying in remote villages and providing healthcare services along the way. In 1988 Mitch co-founded Cape CARES, an international medical relief organization that continues, to this day, to provide critical healthcare services to individuals in the mountains of Southern Honduras. When his children were five and seven years old, the family tent-camped for four months through New Zealand and Australia, and then lived with a Balinese family for two months in Bali, Indonesia. An avid sailor, photographer, musician, and cyclist, you'll find Mitch embracing life along the shores of Cape Cod or at times following his deepest passion, touching people's lives while traveling the world.

Mitch invites you to visit www.mefinally.com and www.seeingwithheart.com for more information.

28313294R00102

Made in the USA
Middletown, DE
09 January 2016